CALL FOR GOD

Call for God

KARL BARTH

HARPER & ROW, PUBLISHERS

NEW YORK AND EVANSTON

Translated by A. T. Mackay from
RUFE MICH AN!
Evangelischer Verlag AG Zürich 1965

FIRST UNITED STATES EDITION

LIBRARY OF CONGRESS CATALOG CARD NUMBER: 67-21543

CONTENTS

Translator's Preface

TRANSLATOR'S PREFACE

SOME explanation is needed of the way in which biblical quotations have been dealt with in this translation. Passages from the Old Testament are generally given in the Revised Standard Version and from the New Testament in the New English Bible. However, in order to be faithful to the mood and style of the original, which makes frequent use of verbal resemblances between texts and which occasionally alters Luther's German, I have frequently found it necessary to make changes, sometimes drastic ones, to the English renderings.

I should like to express my thanks to Professor Barth and to my colleagues at Schiller College, in particular the President, Professor Walter Leibrecht, for their help in settling some problems of interpretation.

A. T. MACKAY

Schiller College,
Kleiningersheim-Neckar
December 1966

THE LORD WHO HAS
MERCY ON YOU

27 December 1959

O Lord, our great and kind God! Since you have come to us in your dear son, we may, we want to come to you, to hear your word, to lift up our minds and thoughts to you, and to try to answer you by what we do here together.

We know very well how much separates us from you and how little we deserve to come like this into your holy presence. We dare to, because you invite and call us to come as your children. But you yourself must help us to speak properly about you and to listen properly to you. Do not allow us to be careless and indifferent in this! But do not allow us either to try to be clever in our own conceits and always to know better than you do! Move us instead by the strong joyful tone of your truth, so that it may gather us, guide us to you and lead us with all other men, humble and consoled, from the old into the new year! Our Father . . . Amen.

For the mountains shall depart and the hills be removed, but my kindness shall not depart from you, neither shall the covenant of my peace be removed, says the Lord who has mercy on you.   ISAIAH 54.10

My dear brothers and sisters,

How pleased I would be just now if I could say something cheerful to you, which each man and woman among you could grasp and understand, and which would accompany you afterwards to your cells and on into the New Year to comfort and encourage you. But you know what happens to the cheering words that are meant to pass, and do pass, from one person to another. We have just heard in the text of mountains departing and hills being removed, and in the same way these words falter and fall; they leave the mouth of one person with sound and fury and cross to somebody else, and there they go in at one ear and out at the other. What good have they been? What effect have they had? This happens because we human beings, when we are speaking and listening, are ourselves faltering, failing, transient creatures. Now I want to try to give you some explanation of what the prophet of old declares is God's Word, and in doing so I must indeed ask—and you too must ask—God himself to tell us once again what is said there, and to say it so that we may and must hear and understand it.

'God', I've just said. Yes, it's true, isn't it, that when we come to church, whether it's to the Cathedral or to this chapel of ours, we hear this word 'God' over and over again. Who is God? What is he like, where is he, what is he? One or other of you may be wondering at this moment. What is meant by the word, what does it say to me, what am I supposed to do about it? Didn't a great philosopher who lived here in Basel say that God was dead? Well, things are probably not as bad as that. Even if God were in fact a dead God for many people and sometimes for all of us, that is very far from saying that he is dead. But there is something in it; while the word 'God' is certainly not dead, it is ailing,

ailing badly, because it has been wrongly used and abused so often, because it has become something of a worn coin. Now, however, the very word God does not appear in our text at all. Instead we are told here very clearly who and what God is: he is *the Lord who has mercy on you*.

In the mouth of the prophet, 'the Lord who has mercy on you' means the one who is great and majestic, who is in fact the *Lord*—who shows that he is great, majestic and the Lord by having *mercy* on his people Israel, by freeing this people from Egypt, by leading them through the desert and giving them a beautiful land, by being ready again and again to receive them, lead them and protect them. The people Israel was a small people and, moreover, a bad and at that time very wretched people. By then they had lost everything: first and foremost their very faith in their God, in the Lord who in fact had mercy on them, their obedience to this Lord. Yes indeed, there are such times when men lose faith in God and obedience towards him. And then everything else is lost as well. Israel was lost, together with true faith and obedience; the might and brilliance of the kingdom of David and the city of Jerusalem were lost, together with the House of God built by Solomon; the homeland, the land of their fathers was lost; their freedom was lost. Just one thing was still left to them: the Lord who had mercy on them. He remained, and in spite of their unbelief and disobedience did not stop being merciful to them—or living, acting and speaking in their midst, exactly as he has done through this prophet too.

'The Lord who has mercy on you'—but now this can and must mean something more for us. Not for nothing was he called merciful, for he has in fact shown mercy to this people Israel. He has shown mercy by himself becoming a man in the midst of this people, and so in the midst of all men, by becoming the brother of all men and sharing their bad nature and their great misery, and by becoming the saviour of all men from their bad nature, from their great misery.

I was once asked how it was that in the story of Jesus told in the Gospels—for he, of course, was that brother of men—much is said about the poor and the sick, about publicans and sinners, but scarcely anything explicit about prisoners; that is, prisoners in the literal sense, just as you are here. Well, it is true; at first glance it seems that little can be found. But might we perhaps not be seeing the wood for the trees? Is not in fact the whole story of Jesus entirely a story about something unheard of before, that the great eternal God has entered the captivity of human nature and existence with all that that implies? And was he not, quite literally after all, also taken prisoner by men, arrested, led away, tried, condemned and executed as a criminal? If anyone ever lived who stood shoulder to shoulder with the prisoners, then it was he. And so shoulder to shoulder with them, as the greatest of those who have been arrested, condemned and executed, he has brought to all prisoners freedom, deliverance and redemption. This is what the Lord who has mercy on you is like: this prisoner who sets you free, who sets all of us free.

My dear friends, what about getting accustomed to thinking to ourselves at once, whenever we hear or read this remarkable word 'God', that he is 'the Lord who has mercy on you', meaning by that the one who spoke and acted in the history of Israel and then in the story of the man Jesus and who, alive until our own day, is active in us and speaks to us also? This is God! If we always did this, we would have good reason for astonishment. But we would then at least be on the right lines, as far as this word 'God' is concerned. And who knows, we might then find that this ailing word 'God' was beginning to recover in our mouths and in our ears!

What is said by the Lord who has mercy on you? Let us listen to that now.

He says this: '*My kindness shall not depart from you*'. My kindness! That means—I, the Lord, am kind to you. Not only kind from a distance; I, the Lord, turn towards you and do so not as a mere empty-handed gesture. I, the Lord, am on your side, and more than that; I, the Lord, will now undertake to guide your affairs and the affairs of your life, and make them my own and make them succeed. Because you are so fine a fellow, because you have deserved it? No, no, not for that! But because I choose, and wish to be kind to you and to myself. 'My kindness' means: You are a thoroughly unprofitable servant, but as such I will take even you into my service. You are a most dubious friend to me— often my enemy rather than my friend!—but I will be a good friend to you, indeed your best friend. You are a disobedient child—oh yes, that is exactly what we all are, his disobedient children—but I will be a faithful father to you. That is the kindness that shall not depart from you. But why not? Simply because it is kindness and therefore completely independent of you—because it is my kindness, not man's but God's kindness. Therefore it cannot and shall not depart from you. It may be kindness hidden from you, but it shall not depart from you. It may and must be largely a hard and severe brand of kindness which will sometimes even hurt you, but it shall not depart from you. We are altogether ungrateful bunglers in the face of it, but it shall not depart from you or from me or from any of us.

The other thing that the Lord who has mercy on you says is: *'The covenant of my peace shall not be removed'*. This is connected with the first thing that he says. It is not at all whim or chance; God is not unjust or unholy if he is kind to us who have so completely failed to deserve such treatment. No, he is kind to us because there is a covenant which he has created, a treaty which he has concluded, because in it his eternal will is at work. This covenant cannot be broken, but remains in force; this treaty is kept, this eternal will is carried out. And this was and is his eternal will once and for all decided and carried out: he 'was in Christ reconciling the world unto himself'. Reconciling it with himself! So it is called 'the covenant of my peace', that is, of the peace created by me. So it cannot depart, it cannot be cancelled. Last week a Christmas meditation appeared in the *National-Zeitung*—perhaps one or other of you has read it—in which we were reminded that in the past year man had succeeded in reaching the moon. Nothing could now cancel or alter the fact that the Russians had sent a disinfected capsule up there and that now there it is! But then the writer went on: There is something which is even more astonishing and certain—that God himself (who is at home even further up than the moon and the sun, the Milky Way and all the worlds beyond the Milky Way) has reached the Earth in his might, and that he has left behind there something other and better than that foolish capsule. He has left the covenant of his peace, our reconciliation with him, the one Jesus Christ, in whom this reconciliation has taken place. So then, just because this peace has been concluded, God's kindness cannot and will not depart from us. Because it is founded on this covenant, on this event between God and ourselves that has happened once and for all and cannot again be revoked, and because this covenant cannot be removed, his kindness cannot depart from us.

But now we simply cannot avoid hearing the rest: '*For the mountains shall depart and the hills be removed*'. That sounds decidedly less good, doesn't it? It must have been a terrible thing when at the beginning of the nineteenth century the hill above Goldau in the canton of Schwyz began to move and engulfed the whole village. The mountain indeed departed and the hills were removed. But let us not miss the point: even then, even when we are talking about mountains that depart and hills that are removed, it is the Lord who has mercy on you that is speaking. Even that will not be purely and simply an evil thing, but, even though we are terrified by it, basically a good thing. If mountains did not depart and hills were not removed, then the truth that the covenant shall not be removed and that God's kindness shall not depart would not win a place in our hearts.

So then, let me now say a few more words about mountains that depart and hills that are removed:

Such a mountain is above all the *time* given to us human beings. In a few days it will be the last day of the year and that will mean: Farewell 1959! You are past and will not return. And if anything is quite certain about the coming year, 1960, then it is that it too will have a last day and so be removed, depart and be finished with. Yes, some day, when our time comes to die, there will be a last day for all of us. And some time *the* great last day will dawn, and there will be no more time at all for the whole world. But my kindness shall not depart from you! If we listen to this, then we receive the strength to live in a time that is departing, being removed and passing away, to accept time as long as it is still given to us, to use it, but also to give it up without grieving when, as must be the case, it passes and is taken from us again.

Mountains departing and hills being removed are certainly also the *human circumstances of life* and *world ordinances* as they have come down to us in history from time immemorial and have passed on again. Just like that; they have come and one day gone again with all the good and less good features that they brought to men. There are no eternities in world history: no eternal Germany, and no eternal Switzerland either, as we used to say occasionally in wartime to cheer ourselves up a little. There is no eternal capitalism and there will not be any eternal communism either. But my kindness shall not depart from you! That is what we may hear in the changefulness and transience of human circumstances and world ordinances. If we hear it, we can last out in this time of ours, whatever it may bring us,—and not only last out by merely putting up with things as they occur, but also by playing a part, whether our station is high or lowly, so that each one of us makes his contribution according to his ability, if not for the best, at least for the better. Whoever hears the word about the kindness that shall not depart, can and may do that step by step, without frenzy, yet without fear, in all conditions and all circumstances, as a saved man.

Speaking about mountains that depart and hills that are removed, we may possibly, indeed we really must, think also of people, the best, nearest and dearest *people* who are round about us. Is it not the case that even the best human beings have their limitations? They disappoint us somewhere, so that, whether we like it or not, we must shake our heads even about them. Even those people who were once closest to us can become remote and strange. And even the dearest human beings can one day be taken from us. 'Do not put your trust in human beings': they shall depart and be removed. But my kindness shall not depart from you! If we take that to heart, it will follow that we may learn to be grateful for those people whom we have and to be patient with them just as they are. And in doing so we may surely also think just how much patience we ourselves require and may experience.

Let me mention another thing that departs and is removed: I mean what is called the *achievement* of a man's life. Certainly it is a lovely thing when someone has faithfully performed something in his life, be it great or small. Why should he not be permitted to rejoice at this? I too know such a person, who has been fairly diligent, has written books, fat tomes some of them, has taught many students, has quite often got into the papers, eventually into the *Spiegel*. Goodness! But after all, why not? Only one thing is quite certain: he too has his time and not more than his time. One day others will come who will do the same things better. And some day he will have been completely forgotten—even if he should have built the pyramids or the St Gotthard Tunnel or invented atomic fission. And one thing is even more certain: whether the achievement of a man's life is great or small, significant or insignificant—he will one day stand before his eternal judge, and everything that he has done and performed will be no more than a mole hill, and then he will have nothing better to do than hope for something he has not earned: not for a crown, but quite simply for gracious judgment which he has not deserved. That is the only thing that will count then, achievement or not. My kindness shall not depart from you! By this man lives. By this alone can he live.

And one final thing: Have we not already thought too that the most certain thing that we can have is to have firm, inner stability, a character and even perhaps a firm faith? Certainly that is a good thing. But 'Let him that stands take care lest he fall!' Dear friends, there can be no question that essentially we all live at the edge of an abyss, where the fall into evil, folly and malice in thought, word and deed is at all times terribly close to us. That is true even if we would like to be Christians, and even if we are supposed to be Christians: 'Temptation has often come upon many a pious man unexpectedly'. No, we cannot indeed believe in our characters or in the good in ourselves. We cannot even believe in our own faith. That could only turn out badly. We can and may believe only that God is for us. You can and may believe only that Jesus Christ has died and risen again for you. 'Jesus' blood and righteousness, my only ornament and dress.' Whether I am strong or weak, stand or fall, doubt or have a calm mind, go my way in darkness or light: My kindness shall not depart from you—hold fast to that, let us all hold fast to that.

I have finished. It is the custom to wish one another all the best for the new year; good luck and blessing and health and joyful days. That is right and proper, and let us now wish one another just that, I you and you me. But in the end there is really only one completely good thing that we can wish one another, namely that the word that we have just heard may really lift us up, support, comfort and cheer us: 'My kindness shall not depart from you, neither shall the covenant of my peace be removed'. That holds good, for it is said not by some man or other but by the Lord who has mercy—on you, on me, on all of us. Amen.

.   .   .

Dear Father in heaven! We thank you that we can recognize you, for you yourself tell us who you are and what you want. We thank you for accompanying us over every hill and into every valley of our lives. We thank you for allowing us all to take you at your word and to find and to love the firm foundation and the eternal source of all good in you.

Preserve us from all stupidity, depression and thoughtlessness which might be temptations for us in the new year as they were in the old! Help us to wait, when there just is no chance to hurry—to put up with what has been laid upon us—not to despise the good because we wish for better! Cheer us with the freedom which no man can give another, but which no other man can take from him either!

And now we call to you and pray together: for all who are in this building—for all prisoners in the whole world—for our relatives near and far—for patients, and for doctors and nurses who tend them—for all who are in mourning—for teachers and their pupils and for young people in the years of transition—for those who write in newspapers— for the authorities of our city and of our country—for the statesmen of east and west—for the Christian churches in their different forms— for the people of Israel—for the proclaimers of the Gospel, both among the unbaptized and the baptized heathens in the entire world. You know what is needed everywhere. And we know that with you is help in abundance. Open our hearts, then our hands will not remain empty!

So we offer out thanks and requests to you in the name of our Lord Jesus, by whom you have made it possible for us to stand upon the earth, to see heaven open, and to look forward to the day when he will come in great glory to make all things new. Amen.

YOU MAY

3 April 1960

O Lord, our Father! You invite us, allow us, and so call and command us, to come to you so that you can speak to us, so that we can speak to you.

You know how much we need this. You know where we all come from: from how much error and confusion, from how much unbelief and superstition, from how much worry and despondency. You know our misdeeds and follies. You know too how great a burden of guilt each one of us carries.

Therefore we want to hold fast to just one thing: the fact that you do not let a single one of us fall—that up to now you have led and supported us, and that you are still leading and supporting us, to give us time to look for you and to let ourselves be found by you.

That is what we would like to do together during this hour, too. For that we ask you to grant us your presence, your word and your good spirit. All that we think, say and do here would be false and useless without the work that you alone can carry out in our midst. And as we unite in spirit with all the assemblies of your people in this city and in all the earth, we ask for your blessing upon them also. Give to their witness and ours light, freedom, joy, and then fruitfulness!

Our Father . . . Amen.

Thus says the Lord: I will put my law within them, and I will write it upon their hearts. JEREMIAH 31.33

My dear brothers and sisters, I do not think that I am wrong if I assume that the word *law* has something oppressive and unpleasant about it for most, indeed probably for all of you. I myself, at any rate, am upset every time that I hear it or read it. And there are good reasons for that.

There is only *one* law where things are different: a law which does not cause distress but gives joy, which does not lead us into a strange sinister country, but into our homeland—only *one* law which does not restrict us and so violate our freedom and become troublesome and annoying to us, but rather sets us free. There is only *one* law which we human beings cannot break or evade, but which we can simply keep and fulfil—only *one* law before whose might and authority, before whose eye we cannot run away and hide—Oh yes, you know, there is such a thing as the eye of the law!—*one* law which we cannot wish to escape: just because as far as we are concerned we can only say yes to it.

You see, it is quite a different law from all other laws—different from the Civil Law or the Penal Law, with which, as we all know, one can come into conflict so easily and with such dire consequences—different from all the laws of the state with their regulations and directives thought out and formulated by men, their commands and prohibitions—different too from the law of good society with its distinctions between what is proper and what is improper—different too from what one is accustomed to call the law in man's own breast, with regard to which we distinguish what we consider to be right and wrong—but different too from the natural law which is supposed finally to determine and distinguish what is necessary and what is impossible. All these are good, necessary and, above all, powerful laws, which we have to heed and respect whether we like it or not. The snag is, that they weigh heavily upon one and all of us because when all is said and done they come to us from outside, from some high or remote place, and so somehow arouse in us all the desire to escape from them, to evade them, to bend or break them, to slip away from them as if through the mesh of a net—or, on the other hand, to close our eyes to them and to console ourselves with the thought that real life begins where they, these laws, stop.

The one completely different law is the law of *God*, that is to say if he puts it within us, writes it upon our *hearts*.

Yes, *if*! In fact it is not a matter of course that God does this. If he does, then it is of his free grace which nobody can earn, procure and take for himself. It is promised to us. Indeed it stands before our eyes at a completely definite place—quite clearly, clearly enough even to grasp hold of. But to receive it, to live by it, we shall again and again have to ask for it.

If God does *not* bestow this free grace of his on us, does *not* put his law within us, does *not* write it in our hearts—or rather: if we do not become aware, or are not already aware, that he is just on the point of doing this—then, indeed, his law, his good and holy law, stands before us, above us, opposite us, like the peak of a high mountain which is shrouded in a dark cloud. And then God's law seems in many ways to be only too similar to those other laws, except that, since it is *God's* law, even shrouded in this way, its nature and its effects are much more powerful, more urgent, more menacing than theirs—except too, that there is no way of getting round it.

Just what is it that God's law says to us if he does *not* put it within us, does *not* write it in our hearts? In that case, it says to us sharply and violently and terrifyingly: You shall! Yes, you *shall* see—that is what we hear then—what you have done wrong, *shall* repent of it and, as far as you can, make it good again and then organize your life in a different, better way—*shall* choose the good and reject evil—*shall* be pure, upright and unselfish (and all that, if possible, 'absolutely', as the people of the 'Moral Rearmament' movement proclaim!). And again: You *shall* help others too, *shall* even be a good example to them! And again, you *shall* believe, *shall* pray, *shall* read the Bible, *shall* go to church! You shall, you shall, you shall! That is how God's law sounds, that is what we hear if God does not put his law within us, and does not write it upon our hearts. That is how we hear his voice from the midst of that cloud.

And what is our position then? Well, we may give God's voice this pitiful answer: I was wanting to, but I cannot, I am too weak for it. Or the frivolous answer: I hear perfectly well what I am supposed to do, I could quite easily do it too, but I don't feel like it; there are other things that entertain me more. Or the defiant answer: I too could do it, but I won't—just because I don't intend to put up with this very 'You shall'. And the worst answer will sound like this: Oh, it isn't all that dangerous. I hear 'You shall' all right. And I may well be able to do it, may indeed do justice to what is demanded of me, may indeed succeed in satisfying God who is demanding this of me. But I will now quite simply be building opposite his mountain a man-made one of my own: the mountain of my goodness, my virtue, my righteousness, perhaps even of my piety. And I shall take my seat high upon this mountain of mine and there confront God as his equal. And then surely would he not owe it to me to recognize me, to praise me, to reward me, as I obviously deserve?

But wait: we cannot get anywhere that way. For through all these pitiful excuses of ours, through our frivolity and our defiance and above all through our utter self-righteousness, the voice of God's law continues to sound: that is all worthless, that is all excuse and evasion. But you cannot get away from me. You hear and know perfectly well what you are supposed to do, what I require of you. And this is what you are failing to do—most of all, when you imagine that you are doing it. If you do not do it, however, then you are a wretched, damned, lost man! Well then, in this way we stand or crouch or lie on our backs: under this accusation, this threat, in the whole predicament into which the law of God must inevitably place us, if he does not put it within us and write it upon our hearts. Our predicament is all the greater, the less we notice that we are in it and that it is a great and terrible predicament for us.

Such, then, is our situation without God's free grace; if the law of God speaks from the cloud, if he does not put his law within us and does not write it upon our hearts.

But that is precisely his promise. He wishes to do this, and he will do it. If God speaks in this way, it is something quite different from what happens when one of us makes up his mind and says he will do such and such this afternoon. We do not know what may come in between, we do not even know if we shall still be alive at all this afternoon. If God gives his promise and says: I wish, I shall, then he does what he says that he will do. And something more: what he then says begins at once to take place.

Let us hear something about the situation we are in when that happens. Then the cloud which veils the hill of his law from us is rent asunder. Then we see him in the bright sunshine, just as he is. Then the same law of God tells us something quite different from what it seemed previously to tell us, when we previously claimed to hear it. No longer does it say 'You shall!', but *You may*. What was it that you said just now? I can't? I don't care to? I won't? What did you try there on the hill of your own righteousness, that you built and scaled by yourself? Why are you afraid of me? And why at the same time do you meet me arrogantly? Why do you want to deceive me in this way or that? What is the meaning of this whole act that you are putting on in front of me? So you imagine that you can only get on with me and my command-ment as long as you still think that you *must* obey me! Utterly wrong! Nobody needs to be compelled, particularly not in front of God. 'Fulfilment of a must', as they say in the eastern states, is by no means the obedience which God requires. Obedience means: to be *permitted* to obey, in *freedom*, to obey of one's own accord, to choose the good and avoid the evil of one's own accord.

So it is with the mountain of God's law when the cloud dis-perses, when we are permitted to see him in the light of the sun, as he really is and seems to be.

What then does God want from us? What does his law demand? Mark this: it is indeed a proper law; it demands some-thing from us, it commands and forbids us to do something and it insists on being kept and fulfilled by us. But what does it demand?

What his *command* says when we hear and understand it properly is this: Allow yourself now quite simply to be loved by me, and love me in return. That, just that, is 'the good', if you do it. That, just that, is the root, the meaning, the force of all Ten Commandments. 'Love and do what you like' said a great father of the church. A bold saying, but a true one. For that's what it's like. Whoever allows himself to be loved by God, and on the strength of that may love him in return, and because of this love does what he requires, is certainly doing what is right. That is what is written.

What God's *prohibition* says is this: Just do not resist any longer the love in which I love you and you may love me. For to resist it is evil, sin, the breaking of all Ten Commandments, which brings about all that is disorderly and bad. If you resist it and do not allow yourself to be loved, if you make no use of the freedom by which you too may love, then you may be the finest, the most excellent, the most serious of fellows: yet the best you do and plan will be false and perverted. That is what is written.

Therefore: If God puts his law, this command and this pro-hibition of his within you and writes it in your heart, then you may obey it. Then you *may* allow yourself to be loved, and then you *may* love him in return—love him, God, and as a result your neighbour also. Then too you may go on to change your former way of life, admittedly in a thoroughly imperfect and unsure way and in all modesty; then you may become—not at once 'abso-lutely', but for all that a little purer, more upright, more unselfish. Here and there you may help a little, and perhaps even be something of an example to others. Yes, and something else: then you may also believe, you may also pray, you may also read your Bible, you may even come into church. Ah yes, I hope so very much, that you have all come here because you may come, not because you must. You may: that is the new and true commandment, the law of God put within us and written in our hearts. Simply and straightforwardly it is our freedom to enjoy him, and obediently to do his will.

'But is there such a thing as this?', you may well ask me. How are we to imagine it? Is it a law which, unlike all other laws, does not imply any hardship or annoyance or anything foreign to us, but is the law which makes us ourselves free to enjoy the freedom to be ready and willing of our own accord to offer obedience to God—the obedience which without more ado is well pleasing to him? How does God create and bestow this freedom? How does it happen that he puts his holy, high law within us and writes it upon our hearts so that we may keep it and fulfil it of our own accord? Yes, indeed, only God can create and bestow that. You cannot, nor can I. None of us can. As I said at the beginning: this is God's work and gift to us, his free grace. But that means that this *is* his free grace; he *creates* it, he *bestows* it.

In conclusion I would just like to add the thing that is most important and decisive. There is in fact a place where we can see, see with our eyes and touch with our hands, how God creates and bestows this, how the work of his free grace takes place. We are now entering once more the period when we remember the *Passion*, in which God in the person of his dear son became to the very uttermost, to the point of suffering the death deserved by the greatest of sinners, our neighbour, our brother, utterly one of ourselves: totally one of us, so that we and all men might become his people, in fact children of God. In this Passion story it happened that the cloud which veiled the mountain of God's law was torn open. Here the words 'I will be their God and they shall be my people' became true. In this story the new and true covenant became visible; here is the covenant between God and us as God intends it, wills it and establishes it, in which 'You shall!' is no longer heard. What we hear is something like the hymn which we are going to sing together afterwards,

> 'Loving, gracious, generous, glorious, Lord victorious;
> Mild, munificent, high, exalted, King magnificent.'

'You may be, indeed you are free,' says God, 'since I make you free.' For in this story God, in the person of the one who stands surety for us all, has put his law within us and written it upon our hearts, has set us free to enjoy the freedom about which we heard just now: the freedom to let ourselves be loved, to love ourselves too. This, the story of the Passion and victory of that one man, our saviour Jesus Christ, is certainly not any old story, which cannot concern us once it has happened because it is past history—it has happened once and for all for all of us. In it, if you are willing to understand it properly, has happened long ago the story of all of us, the story of our salvation, our peace with God and one another: the story of our release. Amen.

Holy and merciful God! What are all our words, and what would our most fervent thanksgivings and praises mean compared with what you have done, are doing and will still do for us and with us?—compared with the new covenant, in which we all may already take our place?— compared with the grace by which you will put your law within us and write it upon our hearts? Enter our hearts! Clear away whatever might prevent you! And then speak further with us—lead us further along your path, the only good path: even when after this we once more separate, to return each to his own solitariness and tomorrow to his work!

So further your work outside this building also, and in the whole world as well! Have mercy on all who are sick, hungry, exiled or oppressed! Have mercy on the powerlessness with which nations, governments, newspapers and alas! even the Christian churches, with which all of us face the sea of guilt and trouble in the lives of present-day humanity! Have mercy on the lack of understanding because of which many of the most responsible and powerful of men see themselves driven to play with fire and to conjure up new and greater dangers!

If your word were not at hand, what would be left for us to do but despair? But your word in all its truth is at hand and so we cannot despair, and we may and indeed we want to feel assured, so that even if the earth is moved under our feet, all things in their entire course are in your strong and loving hand and at the very last we shall be allowed to see that you have reconciled us and our dark world to you, that you have already brought its salvation and its peace despite all men's arrogance and despair: in Jesus Christ your son, our Lord and Saviour, who died and rose again for us and all men. Amen.

CALL ME

11 September 1960

Lord, we have gathered here to serve you in the way you want us and command us to serve you: by opening our ears, and our hearts as well, to what you have to say to us about your love and about what you expect from us. But this great work of obedience cannot and will not be carried out by any of us using only his own knowledge and power. Only you yourself can make us free and eager, willing and able to do it. For our thoughts tend naturally to move along quite different paths and our desires drive us, as we must frankly confess, in quite a different direction. So now we can merely ask you and plead with you to be among us yourself at this moment and to speak your word within each one of us. We also pray that you will accompany and guide us afterwards, when we separate once more, and throughout the new week on which we are starting today, so that the life of each of us, even in this building, may be given its proper meaning, and so that we may treat one another with kindness and tolerance, show respect and consideration to one another and, as far as lies in our power, help one another. All this through your free grace which you have bestowed on us in Jesus Christ. We pray in the words which he has taught us to say: Our Father . . . Amen.

Call me in the day of trouble, I will deliver you, and you shall praise me.

PSALM 50.15

Dear brothers and sisters,

'Call me', we read. That reminds me at any rate of someone 'calling' me, on the telephone that is, and interrupting and disturbing me at my work or in the middle of a conversation or perhaps when I am just about to listen to some music. They begin to ask me how I am keeping, or make some request, or tell me a long or short story, and then say to finish off, 'Call me sometime'. Here in our text everything is quite different. In it someone is certainly calling me and interrupting me at what I am doing. But he does not spend a long time asking how I am, for he knows that better than I do myself. And he has no requests to make—what indeed could I do for him? And he has no important story to tell me either, for the one and only really important story begins with the very fact that he is calling me. What is the last thing on the telephone is the first thing here; what is a minor detail there is the main thing, indeed the one and only thing: Call me!

Who says that? God? Yes, *God!* But the word 'God' is used so much and has become so worn, like an old coin, and everybody understands something different by it. And there are really so many gods too! Let's just put it this way: The one who is calling me here and telling me to call him back is the one who is different: who is indeed utterly different from you or me, from us all, from the whole world. He is the one to whom you belong. For you do not belong to yourself but to the one who has created you and the whole world, from the smallest gnat to the planet and fixed star, without whom nothing would have existed and without whom you too would have been nothing at all. Now he, the Lord of all things, is also the one who means well and does good in everything, including his dealings with us, with you and with me: good, even when we do not always understand that what he is planning for us and doing with us is good. He is our father. He is also our brother. He is certainly also our judge, before whom none of us can stand, before whom all of us without exception are guilty and remain guilty, because we do not mean well or do good: in our dealings with him and with our neighbours and even with ourselves! But he is the one who—miracle of miracles!— loves and sustains us for all that, who does not drop us as we would richly deserve—yet who does not let us escape either, who in great patience but also in great severity is present and is waiting for you and for me, whom we cannot get rid of with secret or open defiance or with our indifference, whom we cannot put off with abuse and curses, or with pious words either! We cannot master him, because he is always there first as our master. The one who calls us is the one who is different.

And now this very one is calling you and me also: Adam, where are you? Do you hear me? Yes, you can hear me perfectly well! There are many other people and things that you cannot hear and even need not hear. But you must hear me. And in fact you do hear me. You simply would not be human and I would not be God if you could not hear me.

But what does he say to us if he calls us? By and large, only this one thing: Call me! That is the gracious permission that I give you. But it is also the strict command which comes to you from me: For this I make you; for this you are free. You may, you shall do this—but only in the proper way: Call me in the day of trouble.

In the day of trouble: 'Trouble' is a word that we all understand. Trouble means affliction, oppression, agony that we would like to get rid of but cannot. There is great trouble everywhere: within the walls of this building and outside them, out there in the city of Basel and in the whole world.

But is it not the case that you are now thinking mainly of *your* trouble, your own, your personal trouble which may be small,

or may even be very great, may be slight, or may be quite
severe. And it is sometimes the little troubles which can be the
greatest and most severe. Your trouble may be temporary, or
it may be one that will last a long time; perhaps it simply takes
the form that you must in fact spend so long in this building. It
may be trouble that you have brought upon yourself or trouble
caused by circumstances or by your fellows—your outward or
inward trouble, and there is no inward trouble which is not also
an outward one, and no outward one which is not also an inward
one. God too knows and sees this personal trouble you have and
tells you to call him in this particular trouble of yours.

But do not forget that you are not alone, but only one of many
who are in trouble. If you really think about it, the whole of
humanity is in fact one single great community in trouble. And
this its *common* and *general* trouble—as is growing clearer and
clearer nowadays—is that whereas we admittedly know better
and better how to control the technique of living, we know worse
and worse how to shape our lives as individuals and as members of
a community. That is one sort of trouble which cannot be
covered up, let alone cured: either by Carnival or by the Trade
Fair or by a jubilee, if one is due once again—or by the grandest
Olympiad, or by communism or anti-communism, or by Moral
Rearmament as they practise it at Caux on Lake Geneva, or by
evangelical campaigns, however impressive, like the one we
recently had in Basel. It is a sort of trouble which simply exists,
and breaks out again and again in great ulcers: now in Algeria,
now in the Congo, now in Cuba, now in Berlin. It is the sort of
trouble that is perhaps worst where one does not notice it, where
one thinks one can spread out the umbrella a little and let the
storm come along and pass by—as we do in our dear Switzerland, and as the people across in the German Federal Republic do
with their economic miracle. Now you need not say that this
trouble, mankind's trouble, does not concern you. It concerns you
very much. You too are involved in this common and general

trouble. You belong there also. And therefore: Call me—not only in your personal trouble, but here too, in this, mankind's, trouble.

But the trouble in which we find ourselves lies still deeper and extends still further. The *true*, the *real* trouble we are in, my dear friends, consists quite simply in the fact that man is as he is and cannot make himself any different. He is the cause of his own trouble. He suffers from himself. 'O man, bewail thy great sin', an old hymn says. Man is a fallen, perverted being. It is not a matter of the sins which we have committed and are committing, but of the sin from which all sins come and so of the particular trouble in which all our troubles, the personal and general ones, have their source, just as weeds cannot help growing again and again from a weed root. Man himself is the *true*, the *real* trouble. Anyone who does not know about that does not really know what trouble is: even if he sighs ever so loudly and touchingly and complains about what is causing trouble to him personally, even if he is ever so angry and despairing about what he reads in the paper. Call me in this deep, true and real trouble.

Call *me*. Appeal to *me*—in your own trouble, in the general trouble, and then, too, in the true, the real trouble that you are in. When you telephone, everything depends on dialling the right number. So do not appeal to what calls itself fate: fate is a blind, deaf and dumb idol, from which you have absolutely nothing to hope. Do not appeal to this or that man, even if he were the mightiest and best of men. He too suffers from his own trouble and from the general trouble and from the deep trouble of being a man at all; just like you, he suffers from himself. Do not call on the saints or the Blessed Virgin either; they were all mere human beings too, and were only 'saints' because they called me. And you are most certain to dial the wrong number if you intend to call yourself, to appeal to your own good sense and will, your good conscience, or to insist on your rights. That is precisely the root of the weed! In that case you would indeed only be calling the one who is your greatest source of trouble. Call *me*: the one and only God, the one and only helper. Call *me*. My dear friends, if only we were to hear this '*me*', then the battle would already be won.

But just what does it mean, to *call* God? Perhaps you think it might mean to pray, to pray beautifully, to pray piously, to pray properly? Yes, certainly, you may and must learn that too. But what good would the most beautiful, pious and proper prayer do you if it were not supported and controlled by our call to God, which is neither particularly beautiful nor particularly pious and proper, but which is the most sincere and genuine thing that we can do? We have just sung:

'From the depths of trouble I *cry* to thee'.

Our call to God is actually a cry. It is the shout: I thank you, that you—who are God over, yet also in, all trouble—wish to be and will be my God and the God of all men, of the whole world. It is the shout: I have not—none of us has—deserved to be told that you are, and wish to remain, our God; none of us can help feeling ashamed in your presence. And this shout as well: But I trust you; I trust the promise which has been given to me by the very fact that you are speaking to me, that you obviously want to be on my side and that I may obviously be on yours. And finally the shout: I ask you—'Put an end, O Lord, put an end to all our trouble'—remove all our affliction, remove mine also. Do it by changing, reforming, converting, regenerating us, and me above all. Put an end to our trouble by making a new beginning with us ourselves. To sum up, as the Apostle Paul once did, it is the shout: Father, my father! Our father in Jesus Christ, your son, our brother! This cry is what God allows and orders us to utter. You all know the saying: 'Necessity teaches prayer'. I believe that one must ruthlessly acknowledge that this saying is a lie. Necessity has never taught anyone to pray. But God himself teaches us, and he does it by allowing us and commanding us to call him and to say 'Father'. You need not feel awkward or be affected, you need not be too modest, yet of course not too haughty either, you need not be too pious or too irreligious to make use of this permission—to shout out 'Father' thankfully, humbly, and confidently in your request.

And now we read: *I will deliver you*. When this word 'deliver' appears in the Bible, the meaning is always that God is already present to save, indeed that he has already saved. If God wills something, then he is doing it already! 'Deliver'—that also means: to comfort, cheer, encourage, help. But deliverance is still something more. To deliver means: to tear away, release, redeem, make different and new. Call me in the day of trouble; I will deliver you! Whom? The pious? The worthy? The efficient? The righteous? The great and strong heroes? But who is pious and worthy, skilful and righteous, and a hero into the bargain? Those who claim to be like that are not in the habit of crying to God. And God saves only those who do cry to him. As we read in another psalm: 'The Lord is near all of us who call him—all who call him in truth'. He is near all of them as saviour, and is their saviour because he is near them: the utterly poor, utterly sick, utterly needy creatures who can do nothing else but cling to him, and wish to cling to him, and have no other choice open but this: to cry to him. Yes, he saves people like that, he has already saved them. They are supported by him even in their trouble, and are already being lifted out of their trouble by him. Though still sinners, they are already righteous—though still sad, already joyful—though still dead, already alive—though still on earth, already in heaven. For with those who are in this position, who call God thus, God, the Saviour himself, has associated in Jesus Christ, his dear son, who as the Lord of glory finally shouted these very words on the cross: My God, my God, why have you abandoned me? God has already in fact made them different, those people who shout in this way, like Jesus and with him;

God has made them new men in Jesus, this one man: made them citizens of a new world, in which he wipes away all tears from their eyes, and sorrow, tears and crying shall be no more. 'He that spared not his own Son, how shall he not with him also freely give us all things?'

And now there remains only the last and best thing: *And you shall praise me.* The meaning is not: you should, you ought to, but: you *are going* to praise me! You—me? *You,* little, wicked, dejected, sinful man in your great trouble—*me,* the great, holy, glorious and righteous God? Yes: you shall, you are going to praise, extol and glorify me. How? Well, just like this: you call me and I become your saviour as you call. Wherever that happens, I am praised, extolled and glorified. That, just that, is all my glory. And it will be present in your life. In your life it will come about that you become my witness, a tiny reflection of my great light in this dark world, in this dark century. It cannot be any different: simply because you call me and I save you, you become this witness, you become this reflection. You? Yes, indeed, you! Us here? Yes indeed, us here, the congregation in the prison!

With this promise we may, we want to, go to the Lord's Supper. Even what we do there cannot be anything other than a single, communal, hopeful call and shout of thanksgiving, humility, confidence and pleading. If we celebrate the Lord's Supper in this way, then the name of God will be kept holy here and now. Then at this hour and in this hall God's kingdom will appear. And then among us and by us the will of God will be done in earth as it is in heaven. Amen.

O Lord our God, our Father in Jesus Christ! We turn once more to you, as you have allowed us and commanded us to do. Be and remain from this day forward what you have been to us in your great might and

mercy up to now, and still are today! If you enlighten us, we are en-
lightened: if you awake us, then we are awake. If you convert us, then
we are converted.

And now we also earnestly ask you to be manifest and active, in your
kindness and your severity, among all other men: among the young and
the old, the sick and the healthy, the mighty and the weak, the Christians
and the non-Christians, the responsible spokesmen and leaders of the
people in east and west, and also among the countless thousands who
listen to them and follow them and so share responsibility for what
happens and what may still come about. All of them, all of us are in a
time of trouble from which you alone can save us, and you are willing
to save us. All of them, all of us are meant to praise you, to give you
the honour. Let them, let all of us, remember and realize that in the blood
of your dear son shed on the Cross you have reconciled and united them
and us and this whole poor world of ours with you and with one another: that our salvation is near us in him and that you have poured out
your Holy Spirit over all mankind, so that he may make us alive too!
Amen.

MY TIME IS SECURE
IN YOUR HANDS

31 December 1960

O Lord, our father! We have gathered here on this last evening of the year because we would not like to be all alone, but would rather be with others and be all together united with you. And now we long to hear something better than the things that we say to ourselves in our own hearts or that here and there somebody whispers or shouts into our ears, or that we can hear on the radio or read in books and newspapers. From all that we cannot live at all. We would like to hear your word, hear you yourself, your consolation, your admonition. We believe that you are alive among us and are anxious to give us the things we need, things that we do not have and cannot take for ourselves. For that we thank you and ask you now for only one thing, to collect our scattered thoughts, first of all to get rid of the defiant, confused and stupid things that might distract us, so that we may now once more be as attentive to you as you in your inexhaustible kindness, year in and year out, are attentive to all of us. Our Father . . . Amen.

Dear brothers and sisters,

I once had a good friend whom I shall never forget. He was a French minister and professor. At the New Year of 1956, just five years ago now, he preached in a reformed church in North Africa on this text: 'My time is secure in your hands'. It was a very warm, meaty sermon, stirring and alive. When I read it again a day or two ago, I found that it was so good that for a moment I wondered if I should not simply bring it with me and read it to you. It was also this man's last sermon: five days later, when he had returned to Paris, he died quite unexpectedly. How do I know that today's is not my last sermon, too? How do you know that it is not the last one that you will be allowed to hear? How do any of us know that we shall still be here in a year, or even in five days? 'In the midst of life we are surrounded by death.'

'My time is secure in your hands'—that certainly also means: My time does not belong to me; it is only lent to me, and can at any time be recalled and taken from me. And then I shall be asked: Who were you in your time? What have you done with the time that you were given? What shall our answer be then? Excuses, pretexts and apologies will be of no use to us then. For he—the one in whose hands our time is secure—will then answer. And everything will depend for us on how he answers. And if there is anything left for us to mention, then it can only be this one thing:

> Jesus' blood and righteousness,
> My only ornament and dress,
> In heaven shall keep me from all fear,
> Before my God when I appear.

That and that alone. It might be well worth considering this, too. Now that we are gathered here together, it will certainly be useful for us to reflect on this truth and to allow this truth to be said to us—as is necessary for all of us.

But now, first of all, I would like to make clear something quite different:

The text does *not* say: Our human time—what we call time— is secure in the hands of God. God is its Lord, it starts with him and ends with him. That would indeed be very fine and very true. It would be an important point to make in a good religious lecture, and would give us beneficial information about ourselves and our times and about God. Why, then, should we not listen to it?

The text from the psalm says something different: '*My* time is secure in *your* hands'. Do you notice the difference? As it stands this sentence is an address, a fragment from a story: not from a story which we can listen to or read or watch in the cinema or on television or in the theatre, but a fragment from a story in which we ourselves may, and must, be present and in- volved. I am in it with my time and God is in it, and obviously he has said something to me, and now it is my turn to speak; now I may and now I must say what I know. Not something about time in general, but about *my* time, and not something about a great stranger who traditionally bears the name 'God'. Certainly not something *about* God (it is always dangerous when we men talk *about* God!), but something *to* God, who is facing me in person: to God, whom I know, and who above all knows me too, and to whom I can speak as a friend just as he speaks to me as a friend—who is now waiting for this very thing, for me to speak with him, to him.

Such is our situation on this New Year's Eve, if we place ourselves under this word. We find ourselves in the middle of this story, of this conversation. Once again: Here we are in our time and here in person is God, who (for instance at Christmas) has spoken to us in all sorts of ways, whom we now may and must answer, to whose face we may now declare and confess how things are with us: that *my* time is in *your* hands.

'*My time*'—what is it? Well, my time is quite simply my life-time, my past from my birth, and my future right to my death, and in addition that most remarkable thing: my present, the constant transition from past to future, the present moment, which continually comes and continually passes—this moment this evening at the end of the year 1960, quite close to the arrival of the year 1961. Our lifetime is the space which is granted to all of us, the opportunity which is offered to all of us, for living. A restricted space, a single fleeting opportunity for living! For when death comes, we no longer have this space; it is past, together with the opportunity. This lifetime of mine, short or long, is secure in your hands!

'My time', however, means more than that. The word translated by 'my time' really means 'my destiny'. My time then is my life story: what takes place in my lifetime—everything that I have done and left undone and shall still do and leave undone, perhaps even what I am doing or not doing at this very hour. My time is my whole life story, with all that I have endured or accomplished and perhaps shall still endure or accomplish—my life story with each and everything that I was and am and shall be. This life story of mine, this is secure in your hands!

Finally, one can sum it all up and simply say: 'My time'—I am my time! I who have lived in it, and am living in it and would like to live a little longer in it—I myself with all that I understand and do not understand, that I can and cannot do, with my strong and my weak sides, with my good and my less good qualities. I am my time, I myself, with my high vocation to love God my Lord with all my heart, with all my soul and with all my might, and my neighbour as myself. But I too am my time, I myself with the abyss of deceit and perversity that is in me. And so then: I, just as I was, am and shall be—as you very well know—secure in your hands.

It is worth while looking rather more closely at the word '*secure*'. My time does not lie around somewhere like an attaché case which someone has forgotten or lost in a tram or somewhere else. It does not roll along like a skittle-ball hurled by some unseen hand. It does not tremble like an aspen leaf in the wind. It does not totter and stagger along like a drunk man. It is secure. It is held. It is carried. It is safeguarded. It is not secure because I am perhaps such a steadfast fellow: after all, none of us is that. It is secure because it is in God's hands. What is in God's hands is secure. So my yesterday is secure, my today, and my tomorrow, with everything that belongs there, whether hidden or open to view. So my time, my life story, I myself have been secure by God's decree for a long time, from long before I was born and so from all eternity. And it will continue secure: not only until my death, but beyond it, for ever. Nothing, nothing at all of what came then and still comes into existence and now is, will ever be lost, forgotten or obliterated. I am, I shall live, though I were dead, because my life is secure in God's hands.

But now at last we reach the crux of the matter: 'My time is secure *in your hands*'. If something is in somebody's hand, then we may assume that it belongs to him for the moment, that until further notice he is needing it and using it and, chiefly for that reason, is taking care of it. But we are not talking of just anybody's hands, but of your hands, the hands of God. If my time is secure in your hands then it belongs to you from beginning to end, and you will need it and use it. And then what will happen will be that you will look after it again and again, and me, too without limit and without ceasing.

My time is secure in *your* hands. Not in the hands of a dark, unfeeling fate, at which one could not help shuddering and feeling afraid, with which one might argue and struggle, with which one would have to keep up a running battle inwardly and outwardly.

With fate I could come to terms. With you, my God, I cannot make terms but only take counsel.

My time is not in the hands of any great or humble man either, against whom I would like sooner or later to rebel, and from whom I would like to free myself slowly or gradually.

And the most important thing: My time is not in my own hands. It is a real piece of good fortune that I am not left to my own resources as a celebrity whose wisdom I would have to admire and respect but also finally doubt, at whose follies I would really have to be afraid at every moment. It is good that I am not my own master, that my time is not in my own hands. But my time, my life-story, I myself, am secure in your hands.

Yes, you may ask me, but does God have hands? Yes indeed, God has hands, quite different ones from these claws of ours, much better, much more skilful, much stronger hands. What does it mean to say: God's hands? Let me put it this way first of all: God's hands are his deeds, his works, his words, which, whether we know it and want it or not, surround and embrace, bear and sustain us all on all sides. But after all, that could be said and understood merely figuratively, symbolically. There is a point where the figurative and symbolic ceases, where the question of God's hands becomes quite literally serious—that is, where all the deeds, works and words of God have their beginning, middle and end: 'Your hands'—these are the hands of our Saviour Jesus Christ. They are the hands which he held outstretched when he called: 'Come unto me, all you that labour and are heavy laden, and I will give you rest.' They are the hands with which he blessed the children. They are the hands with which he touched the sick and healed them. They are the hands with which he broke the bread and shared it out to the five thousand in the desert place and then again to his disciples before his death. Finally and above all, they are his hands nailed to the cross, so that we might be reconciled to God. These, my brothers and sisters, these are the hands of God: the strong hands of a father, the good, soft, gentle hands of a mother, the faithful, helping hands of a friend, the gracious hands of God, in which our time is secure, in which we ourselves are secure. Of him, of this our Saviour, it is in fact said that time was fulfilled by his coming, meaning that in him time—all time and so also the time of each one of us—has received its meaning and its direction and its goal. Let us leave it at that: in your hands—in the hands of your dear son—my time is secure, my life is secure, and I may be secure. He, your dear son, has indeed said: 'None shall pluck them from my hand'. Just listen: No one, no man, no angel and no devil, not even my sin and my death! No one can and shall pluck them from my hand.

In these divine hands of yours I am hidden, I am kept, I am preserved, I am saved. In these hands of yours my year 1960 was secure, with all that it brought me and took from me, with all that, after a fashion, I was and did. Because this is how things are with this year now passing, it was at all events a year of salvation, a year of grace. Just in case we have not felt or noticed this, let us tell ourselves in this its last hour: it was a year of salvation and grace, because it was secure in your hands. My year 1961 will also be secure in these hands of yours, with all that may take place or not take place then and with whatever I shall be and do, whatever I may find easy or difficult, perhaps even very difficult. It will not just be any year, but again it will be your year, a 'year of the Lord'. And this hour in which we now gather is secure, for it is subject to your grace and control, our mysterious present is secure, between past and future: the secret of this moment. Do you know what its secret is? The call, whether soft or loud, which at this very moment is being directed towards all of us: 'Today, today when you hear his voice, do not harden your hearts.' Because my time, because this very hour is secure in your hands, it is therefore for me, for you, for all of us, the hour of decision.

.   .   .

I come to a close with a word of advice or a request: How would it be, if we—each man and woman among us—tonight, before we went to sleep, were to say once more to God, aloud or softly, what we heard just now: 'My time is secure in your hands'? If that were our last act in the old year, then its ending would be marked by our telling the truth. For this is the truth! 'My time is secure in your hands!', and God is waiting for us to tell the truth at last—even in this last hour. What an ending to the year that would be!

And how would it be, if, tomorrow morning, when we awaken, we were to say, again aloud or softly, exactly the same thing: 'My time is secure in your hands'? Our first act in the new year would then be to tell the truth once more, looking now to the future. God is indeed waiting for us just to begin to tell the truth, and this is the truth: 'My time is secure in your hands'. What a beginning to the year! Yes, what about it? What about that for an ending, what about that for a beginning! Amen.

O Lord, our Father! You are telling us today as you did yesterday, and will tell us tomorrow as you are telling us today: that you have always loved us and so have drawn us towards you simply out of kindness. We hear you, but it is for you to make us hear you properly. We believe you, but it is for you to help our unbelief. We would like to obey you, but it is for you to put an end to everything that is too soft or too hard in us, so that we may really obey you properly. We trust you, but it is for you to banish all phantoms from our hearts and minds so that we may trust, joyfully trust you to the uttermost. We flee to you, but it is for you to let us abandon sincerely what must be abandoned and look to the future and walk with serene confidence.

Help in this task all those who are in this building—and all who are erring, despondent, embittered, despairing in this city and in the whole world—all other prisoners—patients in hospitals and mental homes—those who are in positions of responsibility and authority in poli-

tics—*teachers and educators and the young people entrusted to their care—churches of every kind and denomination, that they may guard and spread abroad the pure light of thy word!*

Near and far we see so much that might make us sad and discouraged, perhaps angry or indifferent too. But with you is order, peace, freedom, joy in perfection. You have been our hope and the hope of the whole world in the old year, you will be our hope in the new. We lift up our hearts—no, you must lift our hearts up to yourself. Now, to you, the Father, Son and Holy Spirit, be honour: as it was yesterday, so it is today and shall be tomorrow and for ever. Amen.

THE BRIEF MOMENT

Easter Day, 2 April 1961

O Lord God, our Father! You are the light in which there is no darkness—and now you have lit for us too a light that cannot be put out again, that will at the very last drive away all darkness. You are love without coldness—and now you have loved us too and made us free to love you and one another as well. You are the life that mocks at death—and you have opened for us too the way to such eternal life. In Jesus Christ, your son, our brother, you have done all this.

Do not allow us—do not allow any one of us, to remain apathetic and indifferent to this gift and revelation of yours! Let us on this Easter morning at least perceive something of the wealth of your goodness entering our hearts and consciences, enlightening us, raising us up, comforting and admonishing us!

None of us is a great Christian; we are all quite humble ones. But your grace is enough for us. Arouse us then to that small degree of joy and thankfulness of which we are capable— to the timid faith which we can muster—to the imperfect obedience which we cannot refuse you— and thus to the hope of the greatness and wholeness and perfection which you have prepared for us all in the death of our Lord Jesus Christ, which you have promised us in his awakening from the dead! And now we ask you that this hour of worship may serve that end. Our Father . . . Amen.

For a brief moment I have abandoned you, but with great mercy I will gather you. In the moment of wrath I hid my face from you, but with everlasting love I have had mercy on you, says the Lord, your redeemer. ISAIAH 54.7-8

My dear brothers and sisters,

'With great mercy I will gather you'—you poor, scattered people, you poor scattered man: I will gather, and assemble you where you belong. That is the Easter message, its pledge, its promise. And 'With everlasting love I have had mercy on you'. That is the story, that is the event of Easter Day. Not by a chance whim or coincidence, but with everlasting love, as an unchangeable gift, on Easter Day God had mercy on his dear son; he honoured him, he confessed him, brought him forward as his son, our Lord, by snatching him from the death that rules over all men, from the grave that awaits all of us, and in this way unmistakably proclaimed him to be the Saviour of all men.

He had mercy on him—and through him on the unfaithful, rebellious unfortunate people Israel—and through him, through his son, our Lord Jesus Christ, on all the erring and confused human race—and again through him on you and me also, on each one of us in his particular perversity and forlornness. What God *did* on Easter Day was to have mercy on us in Jesus Christ. And what he *said* to us on Easter Day is the Easter word that we may now hear: that he wishes to, and will, gather us and assemble us, to share the grace which he showed to Jesus Christ.

But we would not understand the glory, the joy and the hope of Easter Day if we were now to refuse to think back to Good Friday, which came before that day. What happened on Easter Day was the explanation, the revelation, of the mystery which took place earlier on Good Friday. Our name for Good Friday means 'day of mourning'. Because the glory of Easter Day was the explanation and revelation of what happened on Good Friday, 'day of mourning' is not really a good name for this day. Nevertheless, the eternal grace with which God, in the awakening of Jesus Christ from the dead, had mercy upon him, was meant in fact for him, the Son of Man, who was crucified on Golgotha and perished miserably on the Cross—was meant through him, for the people Israel hurled from the highest heights to the deepest depths—was meant, and is once more meant, through him, for the human race whose story from the beginning right to the present day was, and is, a story written with so much blood and so many tears. And so God's eternal grace was meant, and is meant, for each one of us, not in his cleverness, goodness and skill, but in the last depths of hopelessness at the senselessness of his existence, which could make his day of life a day of mourning indeed. If a Good Friday without an Easter could in fact only be called a day of mourning, then an Easter Day without a Good Friday could only be a day of empty festivity, which unfortunately it has indeed become for so many people. Let us celebrate it properly, and in this way remember the death of him who rose from the dead today.

What was it like on Good Friday? What was the moment like which God, according to the word of the prophet, calls a brief moment—utterly terrifying, yet quickly passing, because it was overtaken and conquered by his eternal grace? The evangelist describes it like this as the crucial point in the Passion story: Darkness fell over the whole land from midday until three in the afternoon; and about three Jesus cried aloud, saying, 'My God! My God! why have you abandoned me?' And later: 'Jesus again gave a loud cry and breathed his last'. People have often been surprised and shocked at the way in which Jesus shouted out this question in these particular words and in this particular way as he was dying, when he had begun his journey to this place with prayer and full preparation. Then he said, 'Not mine, but your will be done'; now, 'My God, my God, why have you abandoned me?' But we must not alter this cry; we must hold fast to it, take it with utter seriousness: Jesus did in fact shout out that question in that way at that point. At that moment he literally could not help saying to himself and hearing: I, God, have abandoned you, Jesus, for a brief moment. In this moment of wrath I have hid my face from you, my dear child. What God did there was indeed terrible: this abandoning, this hiding of his face in the moment of wrath—not from some evil-doer, but from the only really pure, holy and faithful man—his own dear son. It could not have been, and certainly was not, his response to the fact that Jesus had abandoned him. The truth is that simply by not abandoning God, by being always obedient to him, Jesus was determined to let only God's will be done. He set out and walked along the path which could only lead him, and did in fact lead him, precisely to this point, to the bitter end, where God wanted to, and could only, abandon him, and actually did abandon him. That was the brief moment, that was what happened on Good Friday.

What kind of a path was it which led him to this: into the horror of this brief moment? My brothers and sisters, it was Jesus' path, God's path to *us*: into the dark place, where Israel belonged because of her great, wicked unfaithfulness—where all the human race belongs because of its constant coldness and rebellion in the face of its Creator and Lord—where we all belong, because of and by the very fact that we have abandoned God, and abandon him again and again. Sent by his father, Jesus set out and came to us and so to this place where God is angry and hides himself. And the will of the Father was done precisely in that he followed this path and so entered our godforsakenness. For what reason? It is simple and clear: in order to be for his people Israel, for the whole of mankind, and in place of each one of us, the one struck down by God's wrath and abandoned by God—so that apart from him no one need suffer in the same way. He entered this condition of godforsakenness which would have been our due, to take it upon himself, to bear it and, in the divine power granted to him, to remove it, so that it would not be necessary, or permissible, or possible for it to come our way again. He shouted out the question 'My God, my God, why have you abandoned me?' so that we would not have to ask the same thing again, so that it would no longer be right and inevitable and necessary for any man to shout out the same question as he shouted out there. Why is it superfluous and forbidden for all of us? Because he has done it once and for all in our place. It has already been done: he was there in place of us. He was there in our dark situation, he had to shout out the question that he asked there.

That, then, was Good Friday, the brief but terrible moment— but let us put it a much better way: the great, eternal moment— that meant salvation for the world and for us all. That was the light of Good Friday which then on Easter Day was uncovered and made visible and plain. That was the Yes which God spoke to him as he awakened from the dead, and spoke to his obedience, to his faithfulness—and through him to his people Israel, to all men and so to each one of us—in that brief moment. He really did that already on Good Friday, in that brief moment. Or was it not already God's Yes to the whole world and so also to us which was spoken when God commanded this one man, his dear son, to set out upon this dark path for our sake? And has he not already—in that way, even at the darkest point that this very path led to—said No to our godforsakenness? What happened on Easter Day was nothing new: it was simply the flaring up of the light already lit in that darkness and at first shrouded by it; it was the uttering of the great Yes which God said to us there and of the great No which he said to our godforsakenness there, which became fact and reality there.

And now we may celebrate Easter. What does it mean to celebrate Easter? It means: to see this light of Good Friday. It is there, it is shining, it is waiting only for our eyes to see it. We may, we must, we want to open our eyes, to see it. To celebrate

Easter means: to hear the Yes and the No which God has spoken in what he did on Good Friday: the Yes to all of us and the No to our estrangement from him, which is our misery.

It was certainly the case in the whole history of Israel that the great shadow of godforsakenness lay over this people. And it is certainly the case that we cannot look closely at the history of the world up to the present day, that we cannot read a newspaper or listen to a radio, without being reminded of the great god-forsakenness of human existence. And quite certainly there is no human life, not even that of a single one of us, in which there are never moments, indeed hours, days, weeks, perhaps years, during which we seem to have the feeling, or think we cannot get rid of the idea, that God has perhaps abandoned us—us who have abandoned him so often and who are always abandoning him again and again. I wouldn't like you to misunderstand me: I am not leaving myself out, but including myself when I say this. In my lifetime I have been a parish minister for twelve years and a professor of theology for nearly forty years now, but I have again and again had hours and days and weeks—and have them continually—during which I feel myself abandoned by God, during which I seem to hear him saying to me: I have abandoned you. I have hidden my face from you in wrath, because you have abandoned me. So then: we are all one in this matter, dear friends, and none of you should imagine that his situation in this respect is any different from mine. But we are one and all mistaken if we feel and think like this, however grim and serious our mood might be. According to the Easter story and the Easter message, in the light of Good Friday, godforsakenness can only be a confused memory, a bad dream now. It could very well be true—but it is not true, for you, for me, or for any of us, that God has abandoned us. The truth—certainly not the truth of our restless hearts and our oppressed consciences, but the truth of Easter Day, like the truth of Good Friday—is this, that God holds us fast, whoever we are and whatever our situation, whatever we may feel and think, however difficult our mood may be today and tomorrow, because, and by the very fact that, we have once again abandoned him and continually abandon him. He is present, he does not abandon us, even when we cannot help thinking ourselves abandoned. And his countenance is shining for us even when we think with good reason that we cannot see it anywhere. The truth is that he is completely and utterly ours and that we may be completely and utterly his. That is the Easter message. And celebrating Easter means that we should submit to this Easter truth.

Who speaks like this? Who may dare to speak so boldly? I confess freely and frankly: I would not dare to of my own accord; it would not enter my mind at all to speak to you and to myself so boldly! But God himself has spoken just as boldly to the whole world, and so too to us, in revealing the secret of that brief moment. Thus says the Lord, your redeemer. Amen.

O God, the one God, our only God, strong in your grace, holy and glorious in all your doings! We come once more to you as those who have nothing to offer you but the confession that we would like to live by your great and liberal mercy. We thank you for inviting and encouraging even us to venture on this path. You do not forget us—only ensure that we do not forget you. You do not grow weary—only ensure that we do not grow drowsy. You choose and command what is fitting and beneficial for each one of us—only keep us from wilfully following our own desires and choices.

But we would also like to bring before you here in our prayers the desires, questions and needs of our many fellow beings. Remember all those who are imprisoned in this building or elsewhere! Remember too our relatives near and far! Comfort and revive all who are sick in body or soul, all the needy and especially those who are without human friends and helpers! Help refugees and exiles and all those who suffer injustice anywhere in the world! Teach those whose task it is to teach, and govern those who are called and destined to govern! Provide for your Gospel joyful and bold witnesses in all the churches, in both Catholic and free communions! Accompany and enlighten missionaries and the young churches which they try to serve! May all those who place their trust in you work while it is day for them! Make fruitful all the serious efforts of those who do not know you, or do not know you yet, or do not know you properly! You hear those who are sincere in heart. Give us sincerity of heart so that you may hear our prayers also!

You have been God from all eternity; you are and will remain so. We are glad that we may depend on you and trust you. Amen.

WHAT REMAINS

O Lord, God of heaven and earth! We have come here for the last time in this year now ending to hear together what you have said to us and what you say again and again—to praise you together, as well or as badly as we are able or know how to—to call together to you to give us what only you can give us.

We need forgiveness for the infinite number of things that we have done wrong in this year, and we need light in the great darkness which surrounds and fills us in these its last hours. We need new courage and new strength so as to move on from the spot where we now find ourselves and eventually reach the goal that you have placed before us. We need much more faith in your promises, much more hope in your gracious doings, much more love for you and our neighbours. These are our New Year wishes which only you can fulfil.

So be once more among us at this hour! Show us once more that you are not far off, but near each and every one of us, that you want to, and in fact will, hear our requests: much better than we imagine or intend, as we make them! And be this evening to the crowd of people who are at their wits' end without you, the true God which you have been, are, and will be, to the whole world!

Our Father . . . Amen.

The grass withers, the flower fades, but the word of our God remains for ever.
ISAIAH 40.8

Dear brothers and sisters,

When I was thinking over to myself what I was going to say to you this evening and what the message intended for us all, and so for you too, might be which I had to deliver to you today, three texts from the Bible kept dominating my thoughts. The first is in Psalm 102: 'But you remain the same, and your years have no end'—the second in I Corinthians: 'But now faith, love, hope remain, these three'. And then this very sentence from the Book of Isaiah: 'But the word of our God remains for ever'.

Have you noticed that in each of these three sentences the little word '*but*' appears, and then again in each of the three, large and decisive, the word 'remain'? From the first text we learn that God remains the same; from the second we learn that, strangely enough, something remains in us too, the spark of faith, hope and love which may be glowing somewhere inside us. And from the third we learn that the Word of our God remains and that it remains for ever. I have chosen the third text simply because it stands as it were between the other two and unites and summarizes them. In his Word, he who remains, reveals and creates what also remains in us. The fact that he does this is the great But which is superior to everything transient as it passes away, confronting it with victory, consolation—and admonition.

Thus *the word of our God* remains for ever. I have not forgotten that something different comes before that: 'The grass withers, the flower fades'. We shall also have to speak about that, but here, as so often in the Bible, what comes first can only be understood after one has heard and understood what comes second. So first and above all: 'The word of our God remains for ever'.

What kind of a word is that? What does it say to us now? If only one could put that in a few words! But it can't be done. For the Word of God is infinitely rich and diverse. It embraces

all things in their entirety. It is the whole truth. Who could try to
express truth in its entirety in a few words?

Nevertheless, I am going to try to indicate what is meant here
quite briefly, and in a way each one of you can understand.
Essentially, it is quite simply this: that God is not so much the
'highest', or (as Hitler used to say) the 'almighty', or something
like fate or some sort of final mystery—but that he is *our* God,
so that we human beings—great and humble, old and young—
are likewise not some sort of creatures endowed with a little
reason and a great deal of unreasonableness, but the people of this
God who says of himself: I am your God. It is said in the Word of
God that he has no wish to be God without us, but only with us,
in such a way that without him we cannot be human beings. It
is said in the Word of God that God has created a covenant between himself and us and has kept it until this day, so that we do
not live somewhere out in the cold, but may be, and in fact are,
at home in this covenant. In the Word of God we are told something we cannot understand, that God has loved us all and loves
us and will continue to love us, tomorrow as he has done today,
and the next day as he will tomorrow—as long as we live, and
even when we are no longer alive, with exactly the same love
whether we are wise or foolish, good or bad, fortunate or unfortunate. The fact that we are the ones whom God loves is what
makes us human beings. And since God loved us, he gave himself for us so that we no longer belong to ourselves but to him.
We are not our own masters but his servants, we do not need to
worry about ourselves but are in his care, we do not need to stand
surety for ourselves but have him as our surety. The Word of our
God says all this.

But let us ask once more: What kind of a word is it? Where is
it decisively spoken in such a way that we can hear it? I shall try
once more to answer quite simply: God has said his Word simply
by *doing* what it says. What happened was that he appeared and
worked and acted in our midst as our God. What happened was

that he established the covenant with us. What happened was
that he loved us all, each one of us exactly as he is and as he is
known by God, and that he has given himself for us and so for
each one of us. The word of our God was spoken, and remains as
his spoken word, in the events of Christmas. The way it was
spoken was for him, the great God, to become a man like us, to
become our brother—to make our bad, evil condition his own,
to remove our burden and carry it away from us—the burden of
our sin, the burden of all the error and perversity which presses
upon our lives, in order that it might no longer oppress us. Our
God spoke his Word by making us—and the strangers, the
heathen, and the godless—his children, by giving us a brother in
Jesus Christ. In doing this he has said *his Word* to us. And his
Word tells us what he has done. It is no mere word. It is loud
and clearly perceptible to everyone in the Christmas events: the
infinitely powerful Word of God that embraces and supports
all of us.

This Word of our God *remains for ever*. 'Remain' means: be
steadfast, last, endure, hold out. But in the Bible the word has a
quite particular sound, meaning and emphasis. It is not a matter
of remaining for a certain time, for a while; not only of being
like Christmas candles which are burning just now but will be
burnt down in due course, not only of being like the Christmas
tree which normally remains standing for a little longer in many
houses after the festivities, or like the greenery which I was so
glad to see in your corridors still as I came in. It is not only a
matter of being like the pleasure we have in Christmas presents,
big and small, a pleasure which takes its inevitable course: at first
it is quite strong and lively, but afterwards it can and indeed must
fade, and finally be extinguished. The Word of God remains *for
ever*; for all time, beyond all time. It embraces all the ages; the
whole world, its entire history, and so too the entire life story of
each one of us.

The Word and the Word alone does this. There are other words as well of which one can certainly not say the same. For instance, the words we read in books or in the newspapers or hear on the radio. They may very well be interesting, important, good words, but they will not remain for ever—even if they were the words of the greatest writers and thinkers. That is also true of the most forceful words of Kennedy and Khrushchev (even if he bangs the table with his shoe as he is speaking), of the peaceful or threatening words of a Nehru and a Soekarno, and even, speaking respectfully, of the words of the Pope and our own Swiss Federal President, which we shall be able to hear tomorrow. Let me make myself quite clear: even the words which I am speaking to you just now are not words that will remain for ever, nor will even the best words of all the finest Christian sermons. Certainly there are also some good, illuminating and helpful words among all these. But they can at best only refer to one definite time, and be meaningful for one definite situation. When another generation arrives and the situation changes, then they must be corrected and improved; other words must be put in their place, other speeches delivered, other books and articles written. There is no man whose words are not liable after a certain time to be superseded, put right or replaced by other words. The very most that can happen is that human words might echo, reflect and bear witness to the Word of our God that remains for ever. Not many human words can do even that. And no human word can possibly do more than that.

But the Word of our God remains for ever. It has power, authority and weight, it keeps them and receives them ever anew, without having to be weakened or strengthened, or improved: without it being possible or necessary for this Word to be replaced or ousted by other words. Why does it remain for ever? Because it is the Word of him who himself remains the same and whose years have no end. And because this word was spoken of him not merely once but once and for all. And because it was not a word spoken belatedly about him, not an afterthought, but his first and original thought in which he created the world according to his will. 'In the beginning was the Word, and the Word was with God, and the Word was God. All things were made by him; and without him was not any thing made that was made.' So it remains, so throughout all the years, centuries and millennia it is the beginning, the end and the middle—and so too the beginning, the end and the middle of the life which you and I have to live.

It remains, and that means: it does not grow old; always and everywhere it is young, fresh and new, spoken to each man, in each generation, and for each man and each new generation spoken directly at their situation. It is so rich that it can be and is for each one the exact word that concerns him, a word that enlightens and saves him. And it will remain like this, and be at the same time a word of judgment and mercy concerning everything that we men are and do. It will remain like this in and behind all the little affairs and scrapes that we get ourselves into, as it was before they existed; it will remain like this before, during and after the lifetime of each one of us; it will remain like this before, during and after the entire history of the world. It will remain like this for ever.

So it is that remarkable word *But* which victoriously halts the process of *decay* that threatens us on all sides. Yes, now we must also say: the grass withers—even the most succulent and useful grass! The flower fades—even the most beautiful and fragrant flower. That is true not only of all our words, but of our whole life, even if it is the best, perhaps the most brilliant human life. 'The grass withers, the flower fades.' What was it like in the year 1961, now coming to an end? How much joy and sorrow, how many expectations and fears, how much excitement and re-assurance came our way this year, and have already long since passed away as if they had never existed—to make room for something else that in 1962 will pass by in the same way as we watch? But we also remember this or that person whom we have loved and respected, perhaps even feared and shunned, who this year has all at once died, passed away and disappeared out of our lives. And we do not try to hide the fact that all of us have grown older this year and so have certainly not grown any stronger, that we have had to learn to take things easier and be content, and that in the coming year we shall certainly continue along the same path. It is already like this: our human life is somehow already affected by death, withering and fading, and so we know with uncanny certainty that they will come some day. It is already like this: we are all sailing as it were in a small boat without a rudder, oars or motor on a broad, mighty river, which is relentlessly carrying us along to some kind of Rhine Falls or Niagara. What then? Recently a taxi driver asked me if I did not think that the end of the whole world might be at hand. What has happened in 1961, or has seemed likely to happen, could very easily lead one to this conclusion. And it might well be that the year 1962 could induce us even more to think along these lines.

Just why is this the case? Why is everything, whether great or small, so unmistakably subjected to this great process of withering and fading, and already caught up in it? Certainly not because our existence, our life, our world could be said to be simply evil, bad or dangerous. Together with the heavens, God created our earth too and ourselves as his creatures and, as the Bible expressly says, created them very well. So it can only be that in 1961 in particular we also had cause to be thankful that we were allowed to see this or that little gleam of comfort and encouragement in this period of our lives. And so in 1962 it will certainly still be the case that we shall again be allowed to see certain gleams and so have cause for thanksgiving. It is not for nothing that the great light shed by the word of our God that remains for ever, shines out over all the decay of this world and of our own existence. Everything decays; but it decays in the reflection of this eternal light. Admittedly, simply because it is in this light, it *must* decay. The world goes because its Lord comes. The grass must wither, the flower fade, because eternal life that does not wither or fade is our destiny, God's good will towards us. The ground *must* be removed from under our feet, every day and every year still more obviously and violently than before, so that we may not fail but learn better and better to hold fast to, and to live by, the things that are eternal, and so to live in the faith, the hope, the love which the Word of our God creates in us. All that will be left is what really remains: the Word of our God and his work. For that reason there is this great process of decay, that river on which we are rushed along towards death. It is good for us this way, there is nothing better that could befall us.

I have nearly finished. Some of you were probably here last New Year's Eve and may perhaps remember what we heard and thought about together then: 'My time is secure in your hands'. And some of you may very well also remember that I advised you at that time to say these very words aloud to yourselves before you fell asleep in the old year and again when you awakened in the new: 'My time is secure in your hands'. I could give you the same task today. Today the sentence to repeat would be: 'The word of our God remains for ever'. Yes, my brother and sisters, it would certainly be a good thing to fall asleep today and to awake tomorrow with this very text. One thing is certain: the lives of every single one of us in 1961 have depended on this text being true. And another thing is just as certain: in 1962 our lives will again depend on this text being true. It might well be that the coming year will see an increase in the troubles and confusions that affect our lives and the world— it could bring us the outbreak of a third world war and the big bomb. It could in fact be the case also that the end of the world might come during the year or that it might be the year in which this or that one of us dies, and so for him—for you or for me—it might definitely be the end of the world. But whatever happens, we shall all be allowed to live in dependence on the Word of our God, because it remains for ever: you prisoners here and we people outside, who in our own way are one and all prisoners as well. Whoever does the will of God—and that really means whoever hears the Word of God and holds fast to it as he listens— whoever allows what it creates within him to take root and grow —that is a little faith, a little hope, a little love—such a man remains at this moment and will remain too for ever.

I would like to finish with a verse from a hymn. It does not come from an evening hymn but from a morning one, so it does not look back but forwards, and it runs like this:

> Nothing remaineth,
> God only reigneth,
> Ever enduring,
> Salvation ensuring,
> His Word and purpose shall steadfast remain.
>
> When we're afflicted
> Sore and dejected,
> His words of blessing
> Such power possessing
> Soothe all our sorrows and cure all our pain.

O Lord, our dear God!

Yes, Lord, we are thankful that you remain the same and that your years have no end—that you want to allow us, and do allow us to remain—that your Word remains, in which your heart, revealed to us, speaks to our hearts. Grant us the freedom to hold fast to that and that alone, when everything else is passing away.

And now in this freedom let us take our last steps today in the old year and our first in the new year tomorrow and after that go on into whatever future time is granted us, perhaps a long period, perhaps only a short one.

And so that they may enjoy this same freedom, rouse and enlighten new people where you please—old and young, of high and low estate, wise and foolish—so that they too may become witnesses to the word that remains for ever! Pour the dawning radiance of eternity, as a tiny beam or even perhaps as a great shaft of light, into the prisons in every country, into the hospitals and schools, the council chambers and editors' offices, into all the places where men suffer and work, speak and take decisions, and forget so easily that you are in charge and that they are responsible to you! And pour this radiance also into the hearts and the lives of our relatives at home, and the many poor, abandoned, confused, starving, sick and dying people known or unknown to us! And do not deprive us of this radiance when once our time comes!

Great God, we praise you! In you alone do we trust! Let us not be dismayed! Amen.

THE DOUBLE MESSAGE
OF THE COMING

Christmas 1962

Dear Lord God, you tell us to wait and hasten, keeping our eyes on that great and perfect day when to save us you appeared in the world, among us men, among your people, in our hearts and in our lives. We do not look out into the void, when we look towards this day of eternal light. You have already brought about its dawning by being born as the weak, yet almighty, baby Jesus and becoming our fellow man. And soon now we may celebrate Christmas once more and remember the dawning of your great day.

Allow us—no, help us—to come, grant that on this last Sunday in Advent we may once more consider, think over and look at the way in which we should approach you in the right spirit, since there is now no doubt that you will appear. We ask this so that afterwards our Christmas celebration may not be a mere empty sham, but a bright, serious and joyful meeting with you.

We need to be roused and set going before we embark on such thoughts for the days before Christmas. But only you yourself can induce us to do this in all seriousness. So we pray you not to leave us alone in this hour, but to be present in your might. We call to you in the words which you have placed on our lips through your son: Our Father . . .

He has filled the hungry with good things; and the rich he has sent empty away.
LUKE 1.53

My dear brothers,

During the week I read a sentence in the Migros[1] newspaper 'Wir Brückenbauer' (We bridgebuilders), which I expect you know. It was in an article entitled 'Prisoners' Christmas' (more than that, it came right after a Christmas article written by myself!), and it ran: 'The festival of love and peace is really rather out of place in a convict prison'. What one went on to read was certainly very moving, but the writing was rather feeble, and I am glad that you do not seem to me to be such pathetic figures as the prisoners it described. We must take exception to that sentence. I am not very sure whether the Christmas festival is in place in the Cathedral or the Engelgasse Chapel, where it is celebrated by the best people. But I am perfectly certain that it is quite in place here, and so too in the convict prison. So it was just as well that I had already chosen my text for this Sunday. Listen to it again: 'He has filled the hungry with good things; and the rich he has sent empty away'.

He has done this: he who has taken the side of his people Israel and with it of the whole world—through no merit of theirs, out of sheer kindness! He who was anxious to keep faithfully and fulfil the Covenant which he made with man! He who not only expressed his great love for the world he had created in words, but put it mightily into effect! He who caused his light to shine amid our darkness! He who has given an eternal hope to every living thing! He has done that by himself becoming a member of the human race, a human child, one of ourselves in the town and in the stable of Bethlehem. *He* has done this. It doesn't mean that he wants to do this or will do it, but that he has *already* done it. Listen closely: If you are hungry then he has *already* filled you with good things! If you are rich then he has *already* sent you

---

[1] A chain of Swiss supermarkets. [Tr.]

empty away. That was what happened there. This decision and this separation were made like that when the infant Jesus was born. There the choice was made and yes or no uttered, and for men there was love or hatred, acceptance or rejection. There the hungry were filled with good things, and the rich were sent empty away. And this is the double message of the coming which was proclaimed there and has been proclaimed till now, that precisely this has befallen the hungry and the rich at the hands of God.

The *hungry*—What kind of people are they? A hungry man is obviously one who lacks what he most needs: not anything fine or fancy which he could easily do without, but the bare essentials that he simply must have. And now he has no ways and means of procuring them for himself. Now he cannot avoid going down-hill to his death. Now he is hungry. Now he cannot help being afraid that he will starve.

What he most needs might be a piece of bread and a plate of soup, or, as for so many in Asia, a few handfuls of rice. You will no doubt all have seen pictures of starving women and children in India, Algeria or Sicily. Perhaps even one or other of you has been starving like that. But I imagine that just now, as long as you are in this building, that is not your main problem. What a man most needs may, however, perhaps be simply a life that he considers worth living. What he sees instead is a wrecked, forlorn and spoiled life. Now he is hungry. What he most needs might even simply be a little joy. He looks about him and finds nothing, nothing at all that could really make him happy. So he is hungry. —What he most needs might simply be to be loved properly by someone. But there is no one to love him. So he is hungry.— What if the thing he most needs is a good conscience? Who is there who would not like to have, or ought not to have, a good conscience? What if someone cannot avoid having a bad conscience? Then he is bound to be hungry.—What a man most needs might be something to hold to firmly. But there is

nothing but doubt within him and somewhere despair is in wait
for him. So he is hungry.—What he needs most of all might
be to settle his affairs with God. But what he has heard about
God up to now has meant nothing to him; he could not
make anything of it, and he would not have anything to do
with it either. And now he is hungry in this most important
way.

Of such hungry people we now hear: He has *filled them with
good things*. He has not merely given them something to soothe
them, a sweet, as a mother to her children, or a Christmas present,
cheap or dear—he has not given them something like the
crumbs which fell from the master's table, what poor Lazarus
received. No, he has given them food and drink and cheered
them till they were satisfied. He has, in the words of one of our
hymns:

'rained down from Heaven rivers of love'.

He has made richest of all, those who before were poorest of all.
He has done that by becoming their brother, a hungry man who
with them and for them cried: 'My God, my God, why have you
abandoned me?' He came and stood at their side, to take their
weaknesses to himself, all their perverseness, all their sin and all
their misery. At his own expense he has intervened for them
against the Devil, against death, against all that makes their lives
sad, evil and dark. He has taken all that away from them on to
himself, to give them instead his own gifts: the glory, the honour,
the joy of the children of God. He sent the hungry man away
completely justified, just as he sent that sinful publican to his
house from the Temple. He carried him up as a true saint to the
bosom of the holy father Abraham, like that poor man Lazarus.
He called him into his service just as he called Peter that time
when he had been out fishing for a whole night without success.
He welcomed him as a prodigal son in his father's house: not with

the withering look of a severe schoolmaster but, as we hear in the parable, with the sound of music and the fatted calf.

'These gifts he sends us from above,
To teach us of his wondrous love.
Let all Christian folk rejoice
And praise him aye with heart and voice!'

What kind of a company are these: 'Christian folk'? None other than the community of the hungry who may rejoice and praise God for filling them with good things. Why them in particular? Just because they are hungry and lost and because he is come to seek and to save that which is lost!

But who may the *rich* be who are then mentioned? 'Rich': when we hear this word we probably think first of all of people who have a pile of shares, a big bank account, a lovely house here in Basel or on the outskirts, with original paintings, old and new, on the walls, and probably in addition a holiday home on Lake Lucerne or in Ticino, perhaps too a fabulous Mercedes and a most expensive T.V. set, and whatever other fancy things of this sort there may be. If they feel really satisfied with all this, if they consider themselves consoled and safeguarded by it, if they take it to be the meaning of life to seek after such things, to have them and enjoy them, then they too certainly belong to the rich who are referred to here.

The rich in the sense meant here are, however, really not only those people, but all those, with or without a bank balance and the like, who think they can master life by their own wisdom and power: those who, as we say nowadays, 'know the drill'. The rich in the sense meant here are all the people who consider themselves clever and wise and fine fellows—all who, like the Pharisee in the temple, 'trust in themselves that they are righteous'—all who feel that they must thank God that they are not like this or that rogue, who feel able to announce the good they have done and are still doing—all those who go about claiming that God and men really ought to be thoroughly satisfied with them. Those are the rich who are referred to here.

And it is precisely of them that we read: He has *sent them empty away*. The poor rich! He has done nothing nasty to them. He has not even taken away any of their wealth from them. But he has not done any good to them either. He has just sent them away like the person who has dialled a wrong number or gone to a wrong address in the street. He made them get up and go with bag and baggage. He simply did not find them interesting. He simply could not use them. He simply had nothing to say and nothing to give to them—the poor rich. Yes, it was just the same long ago: what was going on in the stable of Bethlehem simply did not concern these rich people. And right to this day it is a fact that Christmas cannot make these rich people glad. We can even say: the festival of love and peace has no meaning for them. *Poor* rich people, who on the last Sunday in Advent may succeed in hearing no more than that!

But at this point, my friends, we are not yet finished with the double message of the coming. So I ask you to pay serious attention, and to heed and take to heart what has to be considered still.

First of all: not all who appear to be hungry are *really* hungry. Even in the most abject misery, even when seriously ill, even in prison, one can secretly be one of the rich. There are people who are utterly self-satisfied, who are cheerfully confident about themselves even at the brink of death, even in the deepest holes in which men may find themselves. Even in such predicaments there are plenty who trust in themselves that they are righteous! And perhaps worst of all: a man can as it were flirt with his misery and almost take pleasure in confessing and declaring what a poor, forlorn sinner he is. There can be more than the ordinary

type of Pharisees. There are—and I've met the likes of these—
even Pharisaic *publicans*. Whatever pitiful faces they may pull and
however pleased with themselves they may feel under the sur-
face, God has long since sent them empty away, and all the angels
of Heaven keep their eyes tight shut at the very sight of them.
Such fakes, who only pretend to be hungry, need not be surprised
if Christmas says nothing and brings nothing to them. It has
something to say and something to bring only to those who are
really hungry.

Secondly: Of course, it is a fact that the poor rich people of
all varieties *act*—but it can only be an *act*—as if they were rich,
while in reality they too are abjectly poor. With their wealth they
lie to themselves, to God and other people, about something that
does not exist. For in truth no man is satisfied with what he himself is and has: whether it is his bank account or his Mercedes or
his uprightness and his piety. In fact no one is his own master, no
one architect of his own fortune and, whatever the proverbs may
say, no one is his own saviour. By pretending to be something,
and for as long as he acts like that, a man is contemptible in God's
eyes, is one of the people whom God has ignored, has sent empty
away, in order to show his tremendous kindness towards the
whole human race. As long as he does that, he can only watch
God filling others, the hungry, with good things; he cannot celebrate a joyful Christmas; as far as he is concerned the angels have
sung for nothing.

Thirdly: There is therefore some hope even for the rich people
of all kinds who for the time being have been sent away. The
poor rich man should not act as if he too did not lack what he
needed, as if he too was not hungry. He ought to recognize and
confess that he too is not at all a clever, wise and fine fellow but in
all seriousness a very nasty, useless and wretched creature. He
ought to go and stand openly and honestly beside the publican—

the genuine publican of course, not that fake!—right at the point where the Saviour stands beside him too. He ought to be prepared therefore to know and acknowledge only one thing more: God be merciful to me a sinner! In an instant everything would change and be different. He would no longer be a *poor* rich man, but a *rich* poor man—one of those of whom the Gospel says: *Blessed* are the poor. He would then be filled with good things, too. He would then hear and perceive what the angel said to the shepherds: 'Behold, I bring you good tidings of great joy, which shall be to all people. For unto you is born this day a Saviour!' And then he would be permitted to join in the hymn of praise of all the heavenly hosts: 'Glory to God in the highest, and on earth peace, good will toward men!' Do you know the sure sign that anyone is genuinely one of the hungry and has been released from his lying, and so is a man filled with good things, a *rich* poor man? Such a man will have a heart and hand generous to other hungry people of all kinds. He will for instance be not just a little concerned, but vitally concerned, that in India, Algeria, Sicily and elsewhere there are millions who are deprived of bread, soup and rice. Their problem will then also be his. He will then recognize his brothers and sisters in these people and act accordingly. By doing this he would be allowed to celebrate, and would in fact celebrate, a joyful Christmas.

And now there goes out to all of us the invitation to celebrate Christmas. Behold, I come quickly, says the Lord,—the Lord Jesus Christ, the Lord of Hosts, beside whom there is no other God—and he continues: 'Come unto me, all you that labour and are heavy laden, and I will give you rest.' 'You who are poor and wretched, come here, fill the hands of your faith abundantly. Here are all good gifts: here is the gold with which to bathe your hearts.' Come as you are, as people who are really hungry. Do not pretend that you are not like that. And now we can pick up that gloomy sentence which I mentioned at the beginning and stand it on its head: In a building where there are people who labour and are heavy laden, the poor and wretched, those who are really hungry—and therefore in a building like this one in which we are—the Christmas festival *is* in place. Only in such a building! But most certainly in such a building! Amen.

O Lord, our Sovereign and Saviour! Now let us enter the days of festivity without false ideas, but with our hearts open to receive your Word, your promise, your commandment! Our complaints and questions, our errors and mistakes, our uncertainty and defiance, will trouble us even in these days, and trouble you even more. But even in these days you want to, and will, accept us and lift us up as we are, and will say Yes to us if we are willing to be counted among the hungry and not the rich.

Asking for this knowledge, which all men need so much, we come before you to plead for all who are troubled, confused and perplexed: in this building, in our city, in our country, in the whole world—for those in hospitals sick in body or mind, and for their doctors and nurses— for the teachers and the children, big and small, in our schools—for our administrative authorities, for our politicians and journalists—for the Christian churches here and everywhere: that the Gospel of your free grace may be proclaimed more and more clearly and joyfully among the Catholics—and all the more freshly and widely among us Protestants— and may become the salt which the world needs so badly.

And now let us have a good Christmas: let us look forward beyond its fleeting lights towards the perfect dawning of your eternal light! Amen.

WHAT IS ENOUGH

31 December 1962

O Lord, our God, today you have brought us to the end of yet another year of our journey through the time allotted to us. You have made us free and able to take all the steps, long or short, that we have taken. You have been our faithful companion and have governed and guided us. And you were present with your Word, your promise, with your commandment. Whatever you have thought about us, done to and for us, and said to us, was right and proper.

Not so our thoughts, words, attitudes and deeds! Since we can only thank you, we must openly confess to you and to one another how negligent we have been in this respect again and again, and how much we have done wrongly and perversely. We would have richly deserved it if you were to put an end to us today instead of allowing us to enter another new year. If then you treat us so very differently, we can do nothing but praise your inexhaustible mercy. To do that, we have once more come together as a congregation of your people. Our prayer is that in this hour also the proper things may be said properly and heard properly. Give us the faith, the hope, the love which we need for this and which you alone can give us! We ask these things in the name of our Lord Jesus Christ and pray in his words saying· Our Father . . .

My dear friends, that is a very short text—only four words—I think it is the shortest on which I have ever preached. The advantage of this is that you can remember it all the better. It is, by the way, my most important concern, each time I am permitted to be here, that the word from the Bible should stick in your minds and stay with you afterwards rather than my sermon. So for today the text is: My grace is enough. The point of this text lies in its very brevity—it illustrates, as it were, what it describes. These four words are enough. Some of you have perhaps heard it said that in the last forty years I have written a great many books and that some of them are very fat ones. Let me, however, frankly and openly and even gladly confess that the four words: 'My grace is enough' say much more and say it better than the whole pile of paper with which I have surrounded myself. They are enough—something that I am very far from being able to say about my books. Whatever might be good about my books could at best only consist in pointing out from the distance what these four words say. And when my books have long since been superseded and forgotten, and the books of the whole world with them, then these words will still shine on in all their eternal richness: My grace is enough.

And now a second preliminary remark. If you want to look up this text afterwards in your Bibles, you will find that in the German translation of Luther, which is still the one most widely used, the text has a rather different wording from that given by me: the version there is 'Let yourself be satisfied with my grace'. It is very true that you may and must let yourself be satisfied with what is enough for you. But the original wording is better still. Whether you let yourself be satisfied with it, whether you are satisfied with it or not, my grace is *enough* for you. It stands there like a solidly based tower or like the Matterhorn or like the Pole Star round which our whole universe seems to revolve. My grace is *enough*. Because it is enough for you in all cases, *therefore* you can, may and must *let* yourself be satisfied with it, today as yesterday and tomorrow as today. It was enough for you in 1962. It will also be enough for you in 1963.—Let us now approach this fact a little more closely.

First of all a most important point: No man can say to himself: My grace is enough. For no one can provide grace for himself. It is always a terrible error if anyone thinks that he can be enough for himself. That there is such a thing as grace and that it is enough for us is something that each of us can only take from someone else's lips. But we cannot even take it from other men. No human being is gracious and no one is in a position to give grace to anyone else. Long ago there were of course certain high ranking people who insisted on being called '*gnädige*[1] *Herren*' (gracious sirs)—the occasional potentate even demanded '*allergnädigster Herr*' (most gracious sir). And even to this day in Germany one can now and then hear '*gnädige Frau*' (gracious lady) and '*gnädiges Fräulein*' (gracious lady, said to a younger unmarried woman). You will also know words like '*Gnadengesuch*' (appeal for mercy), '*Begnadigung*' (pardon) and so on. But that was and still is essentially nonsense. No man but one has grace to give. From no man but one can grace be expected. So no man but one can say to others: 'My grace is enough'. Only one man can say that. Only from one man can we take it.

We owe this text to the Apostle Paul. But it is he who writes expressly: 'And *he* said to me, My grace is enough for you'. 'He' is the one and only man who had, and to this day still has, the right and the authority to say that to others; the man Jesus who for Paul was not only a holy name—not only an eminent figure about whom he had heard from others or read about in books by others, but a living person who reveals himself to him as the true

[1] The words referred to here are all derived from the German word *Gnade*, grace. [Tr.]

man who was also the true God, as Lord and Saviour of all men, of the whole world, and had permitted himself to be known and who now was going about with him as a king does with his most trusted messenger. He, this one, has said to Paul: 'My grace is enough'. It was a most remarkable, puzzling, and contradictory situation in which he said that to him: amid the dilemma caused by two completely opposing experiences, the one glorious, the other terrible—the one intensely elating, the other profoundly depressing. I ask you to read this for yourselves in the chapter we mentioned. It would lead us too far today if I were to try to describe and explain these circumstances to you. Let us rather just hear simply what the Lord said to Paul in this extraordinary situation in his life. He wrote it down, only not as his own word but as the word addressed to him by his Lord Jesus Christ. In this form he passed it on further. So we too may pay attention to this word as one spoken particularly to us and valid for us. He, this Lord, is gracious, is in a position to exercise grace and to say: My grace is enough—he alone, no angel, no other man, no one talking to himself. But he does not wish to do only that. He *has* said it to us, in 1962 as well. And he will say it again to us in 1963 too. That *he* has said this and says it even to *us* is the truth and the power, the deep comfort and the wonderful encouragement, contained in this word.

If anyone is *enough* for another person in what he is to him, does for him, gives to him, that obviously means that he gets for him and supplies him with what he needs, not more, not less, nothing else. But what does another person like this *need*? What would anyone have to be or do or give in order to be enough for someone else? If we think about this question for a little then we cannot help discovering that at first every answer seems to slip out of our hands.

After all, we need so *many* things, and such *different* things: now *this*, now *that*, big things and small things, necessary and less necessary, external and internal; food for the body, but food too for the soul, the heart, the emotions; something human but something divine also. But what, of all that, do we in fact really need? What would be enough for us if we were to receive it?

Furthermore, we need all those things in *variety*: not only work but also rest and entertainment—not only this but also that pleasure—not only the family but also comrades and friends—not always the same faces but also quite different ones—not only our homeland but also distant places, abroad. Even the most beautiful thing would become dull for us if it were the only thing. So it comes about that many people can only imagine heaven and eternity as pretty dull affairs, because they think that they will have nothing to do there but sing psalms and chorales endlessly. All right: but where in the apparently never-ending film of our life, with all its changing scenes, does the thing appear that we really need? Where is the thing that is enough and that certainly could not be boring for us then?

Another thing: As you all know, we need everything again and again: in never-ending *repetitions*. So it is with the taking of food, so with sleep. If we experience some joy, then we would like to have it again. Once we are comforted, we call out immediately to be comforted once more. If someone has grown very dear to us, then it is not for nothing that we say: Be seeing you. If we have had a certain length of time given to us (e.g. another whole year) then we know very well that it is not enough, that we want still more time (a 'happy new year'). What we really need appears always to be something over and above what we could receive all at one time. But in that case what do we need? What can and will ever be able to satisfy us?

Let us return to what the Lord said to Paul and so to us as well! What is said to be *enough* there is quite certainly what we *need*. No need for anxiety on that account! We shall not come off badly. It is just that what we need and what is enough for us looks a bit different from what we think it is. Paul described it in an earlier passage of the same letter with the strange sentence: 'You will always have ample means in yourselves to meet each and every situation'. That sounds different, doesn't it? It is very different too.

What we need would therefore seem to be something *complete* in which the many different individual things that we need would certainly be contained, but in which they would be secured firmly, properly held together, arranged and refined. That is what we really need. That could and would be enough.

What we need would in addition be something *unique* which in the strange fleeting passage of our years and of their appearances and forms would endure throughout all change, and would give meaning to the change, and make every individual thing interesting and anything but boring. That is what we really need. That would be enough.

What we need would be (and this is the essential quality) something *eternal* which amid the series of necessary repetitions would itself need no repetition—which would be present with us not only once but once and for all, and would remain and be ever renewed: yesterday *and* today *and* tomorrow, in 1962 *and* 1963. That is what we need. That would be enough.

The Lord spoke to Paul about this very thing and he speaks about this very thing now to us also. You now perhaps understand better: that we would never find out by ourselves that this is what is enough for us, what we really need. That we are looking for this thing which is complete, unique, eternal and that such a thing exists and is available to us is information that we can only accept from someone who knows because it is his own kingdom, the kingdom of his might and glory.

My grace is enough, he said to Paul, and he says the same thing to us now.

My grace—that is what *only I* can give to you—no friend however dear, no benefactor however noble, no minister however serious and eloquent, not the whole world. Why not? Because to be gracious and to exercise grace is something that belongs entirely to me and has been conferred on me by God.

My grace—that is what I *want* in fact to *give* you, and another thing: it is what I have *already given* you, whether you notice it and are grateful for it or not, and what *I am giving* you here and now and *shall give* you again and again.

My grace—that is what you have not the slightest claim upon, what you have not earned, what you are not worthy of but what shall be *yours,* and shall *belong* to you without your doing anything.

My grace—that is *myself*: I for you, I as your Saviour in your place—I who set you free from sin, guilt, misery and death, all of which I have taken on myself and so away from you—I who show you the father and open up the path to him—I who let you hear the great Yes which he spoke to you too, to you personally, from all eternity—I who in this way appoint and install you as God's servant and who make you useful, ready and willing for this particular service.

That is my grace. *And this grace of mine is enough.* It is what you really and truly need, and what you, moreover, may and must have. You can hold on to it, you can live by it. You can also die with it. It is enough for you just now, it will also be enough for you to all eternity.

Dear friends, today is the third time that I have been allowed to be here among you on New Year's Eve. And each time, two years ago and again last year, I presented the biblical text that it was my job to explain and expound as a sort of watchword for the way. In 1960 it was 'My time is secure in your hands'. In 1961 it was 'The word of our God shall remain for ever'. And now today, in 1962, it is to be the reverse of what we have heard this evening about what is enough for us: it is to be our *answer* to what the Lord said to Paul and so now to us as well: '*Your grace is*

enough'. My dear friends, say that to him as the last thing you do
in the old year and then again as the first in the new year. Say it
to him softly, shyly, modestly. Who could say it any other way
to him? We are, after all, men who are apparently too proud to
say a thing like that out loud. But say it to him! He hears it and is
glad to hear it from you. He expects nothing more from you and
from me than that we should say it to him as the echo of what he
says to us: 'Yes, your grace is enough'. Amen.

*Eternal, holy and gracious God our Father! The first hour of a new
year is now not far off. You know the good opportunities, and the
problems, temptations and dangers that it may bring us. In every case
it will be you who will encounter us in the changing times and
circumstances. You the inexhaustible source of everything that satis-
fies us, of everything that we need. Let us come near you from
the very beginning and then again and again in childlike, obedient
trust: thankful in advance for everything, because in everything
you are anxious to increase your honour and make plain our salvation.*

*Into your hand we now lay all the troubles and hopes which affect
us as we play our part in the events taking place in the world of our day.
Enlighten the men who bear so heavy a responsibility for the form that
the destinies of the peoples of this earth will take! Rouse the peoples
themselves too so that they do not merely long for peace but also gain
inclination and strength to be active in their pursuit of it! Prevent and
destroy both in the east and the west the self-righteousness whose
continuation and growth could only lead to war, atomic war! Prevent
especially the lying, provocative propaganda practised by both sides!
Give soothing and healing to the millions of individuals who have to
suffer in the present-day situation and also to those who today as in
every age are lonely, poor, sick, imprisoned, and as such are despondent
and sad! And if it may be done without harming the truth, then bring
about in the new year among the community of those who believe in*

Jesus Christ further approaches and agreements between the churches which bear his name!

Now, despite all our weakness, may we praise you at all times, Father, Son and Holy Spirit, as in the past so in the future and to all eternity. Amen.

BEFORE THE JUDGMENT
SEAT OF CHRIST

---

24 February 1963

O Lord our God! We have come here. Here we are. Perhaps only because we wouldn't like to be alone with our thoughts for an hour. Perhaps only because we would like a change from hearing the same old stories we can tell one another or read in books and newspapers. Perhaps only because we imagine that a proper Sunday rounds off a proper working week. But whatever our reason, we might certainly have heard your voice, your call and so be quite right. If we are with you, we are certainly no longer alone. If we hear your word, then most certainly we hear something new and different. If we may celebrate this Sunday with you, then it will be a sunny day at the close of our working week.

You know us better than we know ourselves. With our little bit of faith we don't get far. But hear us as we join our voices together, and answer our prayer as if it were the confession of a rich, strong faith. Step into our midst and yourself speak to us. Open our ears and hearts yourself so that we may be free to hear you. We pray that the speaking, prayers and singing with which we try to answer you may at least bear a distant resemblance to the rather better praise offered by your holy angels. And let the same thing take place wherever your congregation on earth assembles on this day to bear witness to the great acts of your mercy.

This we pray in the name of our Lord and Saviour Jesus Christ and in his words we add: Our Father . . .

We must all be shown up before the judgment seat of Christ.

II CORINTHIANS 5.10

My dear friends, we all know what it means to appear *in court*. I can quite easily include myself too as I say this, for nearly thirty years ago now, in the days of Hitler, in Cologne on the Rhine, I too once appeared in court. I was accused and charged there by a wicked lawyer who said that I had done what was not allowed in the Germany of the day and had not done what ought to be done in the Germany of the day. Three judges sat opposite me and looked at me with serious, suspicious faces. And an able young lawyer sat next me and took great pains to prove that everything was not as bad as all that. Everything took its inevitable course. I was found guilty and sentenced to be dismissed as an unreliable state official and as a bad teacher of German youth. Now that is a long time ago and as you see I have survived it pretty well up to now.

I am telling this simply to remind you about something you know more about than I do: what it is like to come up before a *human* court. In the middle of a lot of people—and with everybody's eyes on him—sits the accused, to be called to account by other people for what he has done. Now they find out what according to human understanding can be shown up about his case. And they decide what sentence according to human judgment he shall receive. He has then to put up with it willy-nilly. Perhaps he can and wants to appeal, which will just mean that he has to come up once again in front of another human court. And then life goes on: for all the people involved and so for him too, the man who has been accused and now sentenced. Other events follow and, who knows, some day he may perhaps be handed out a prize instead of a sentence: of course it's again a matter of human judgment.

How trivial all that is, almost laughable, how it pales into insignificance compared with what is declared to us by the

Apostle Paul here in our text: *'We must all be shown up before the judgment seat of Christ!'*

When that happens life will not go on, to sound the depths or scale the heights. What exists and is happening just now will come to an end then. Everything—heaven and earth in their present, visible form, world history, as we see it just now and judge it, we ourselves with everything that we were, are and shall be—all this will belong to the past, that is, will have passed away. It will even be the end of all human court scenes and prize-givings; they will then simply be things of the past: everything will have become part of one great yesterday. A dream, you might very well have said. Oh no! It was no dream, it was our real life, only it will by then be behind us, settled without hope of appeal, and will have become our yesterday.

What then? We hear: this life of ours, once real, but now completely part of yesterday, will then be shown up for what it is. At the moment it is hidden by a veil. Just now there is much, a great deal, really everything, that we don't see as it really is. We don't even see ourselves as we really are. And others do not see properly either. God sees us properly even now, he sees what is going on inside us—he sees what our wishes and intentions have been from our earliest days and what our wishes and intentions are today—he sees how things were, are and will be between us and our fellow-men—he sees what we have achieved and carried out and shall yet achieve and carry out—he sees who and what we really are. We don't see it like this yet. We see, to use the words of the Apostle Paul, only through a glass darkly, only as if life were a great riddle—and even if we are, or claim to be, Christians, we see only in faith, not face to face. That is the veil. This veil will then be *pulled away* all at once. We shall then be shown up. No part of anything that was present and took place in our lives will then stay hidden: either to our own eyes or to those of other people. Everything will then come to light and be

clearly seen; nothing will be forgotten, nothing vague and
ambiguous, nothing misleading any longer. The whole great
Yesterday of our real life will then be in full view like the pages of
an open book—everything exactly as it has been.

We *must* then *all* be shown up. There will be no game of hide
and seek like the one Adam tried to play in Paradise. The light
that will then start to shine will light up everybody and everything without interruption and bring them into view. Nobody
will then be able to remain a private person, or to opt out, or to
get away from the shaft of light and so from publicity: not even
any of the mass of people who have never appeared before a
human court. And nobody will then be able to make exceptions,
set this or that matter aside with the explanation that it was a
private affair which did not concern anybody but himself. We
may try to carry on like that just now. But then the whole story
will be published and become public property.

Now we come to the main point: when these things are shown
up, we, and our present real life, will come up *for trial*. The light
that bursts in will show if it has been an honest or an untruthful
life in general and in particular, a beautiful or a barren life, a life
lived in love or in indifference or hatred, a useful or a useless life.
A moment of crisis will then arrive. 'Crisis' means separation.
At that time everybody and everything will be separated out just
as if a sharp knife had been used among them. And a decision
about them will be taken with the utmost precision: who and
what we were, and whether we are to stand on the right, that is
the good side—or on the left, the bad side.

One thing is for sure: The judgment then will be divine and
not human any longer; the separation, the decision and the
sentence will be carried out according to divine, and not human,
wisdom and justice. And that means that we shall have good
reason to be surprised how often the first is last and how often the
last is first—we shall be surprised too how often what is important
just now will turn out quite trivial then, and how often what is

trivial just now will turn out quite important. We can depend on one thing: at all events it will be done properly and thoroughly. And we can depend on this too: there will really be a judgment, a separation, a decision and a sentence and it will be decided what is to happen to each one according to the sentence that is passed on him. 'Each must receive what is due to him for his conduct in the body, good or bad'—so runs the continuation of our text. Lastly, we can depend on this as well: there will be no more suspended sentences, chances to appeal, early releases—least of all relapses! We shall be up before the highest judge. It will be the final, the 'Last', the definitive, the eternal judgment to which we shall then come. Life will just no longer go on after that.

What more can we say? How then shall we survive? What will become of us then? Have we anything to comfort us—as we walk inevitably towards this day of judgment? To answer these questions we must note especially once again that the text says: We must all be shown up before the *judgment seat of Christ*. Not before the throne of some unknown heavenly chief-justice, like the one whom many heathen have imagined in fear and trembling! No, but in front of him who has loved us from all eternity and then in his birth in the stable of Bethlehem and in his death on the Cross on Golgotha, and has drawn us to himself out of sheer kindness! Before him in whom God concluded and faithfully kept and fulfilled his covenant with us men! *This* is the one who will be our judge; it is his light, the light of the last day, in which we shall all be shown up—the separation and decision to which we must then submit is *his* work—the sentence which will then be pronounced on us is *his* word. Indeed it is not just *one*, but *the* great, effective consolation, that we are to be shown up in front of *his* judgment seat. Ah yes, but just because it is such a great and effective consolation, it is no cheap consolation!

For let us consider: On that day we shall be shown up as having sinned daily and hourly *against him*, this mediator of our salvation.

He is the one whom we have neglected in looking out for, and questioning, other gods who were mere idols. He is the one whom we have ignored, despised and hated in our fellows, his brothers and sisters—these fellow creatures who are often so troublesome, so wicked, so crazy and always so poor. He is the one, and it is his free grace that we have rejected when we tried to be obstinate and to build not on it but on our own innocence, goodness and perhaps piety. In short, it is as *his enemies* that we have lived and as his enemies that we are now to appear before *his* tribunal. Though this may be a consoling prospect for us, we shall have to realize and admit that we have sinned against *him*; and still are sinning, that we are utterly inexcusable before *him*, our judge. Such a prospect can only be consoling for us if and when we hold fast to this one fact that he has accepted those very ones who have not deserved it of him, that he forgave those who nailed him to the cross and mocked him as he was being crucified, that he has loved us too even as his enemies, and loves us and will love us still. The great, effective consolation when we face the coming judgment is that the judge is the one who has taken our side like this, that we may believe in the one who is like this, place our hopes in the one who is like this, and love the one who is like this. This expensive consolation cannot be had more cheaply than this. But it is to be had like that, at once, completely and with utter certainty.

Let us consider the same thing in a rather different way: It will then become plain that he, Jesus Christ, the true son of God and true son of man who will then be our judge, has already walked along exactly the same road that we all ought to follow to be right: under God's judgment and death sentence, to the left, the bad side, into the midst of the damned and the eternally damned. So it is with us. That is our situation, our proper place, if we remember that it is into our situation and place that he has stepped. Again, the prospect of being shown up before his judgment seat can only be consoling if we realize and admit that that is where we belong, so that afterwards we can hold fast to the fact that he is ready as our judge to step down once more to us, to acknowledge us, to come to our side and so prove to be our one and only, but victorious advocate. The great, effective consolation is that we may recognize and confess this very man, this judge, as our true advocate, believe in him as such, set our hopes upon him as such, love him as such. This expensive consolation cannot be had more cheaply than this. But it is to be had like that, at once, completely and with utter certainty.

That is all. *Fear* of that light and judgment? You have probably noticed that we could have very serious grounds for being afraid in this connection. But if we seize the great, effective consolation and let it be our only consolation in life and death, then the grounds for fear, however serious they may be, disappear. We then have reason for *joy*—not for joy in ourselves, but rather for joy in him, Jesus Christ, who was yesterday, is today and will be for all eternity—reason for joy at the fact that we must be shown up *before his judgment seat*. Must? No: may! Amen.

O Lord, our God and Father, we are thankful that the word that you have spoken to us in your dear son, Jesus Christ, is so strict yet so kind, so humbling yet so uplifting. We thank you for giving us no other alternative but to bow down before you and for making us in this way free and happy to stand on our feet and to look gladly and confidently towards the revelation of your kingdom. Lead us continually by your Holy Spirit to renew our obedience to you in both these ways!

And now we think of the needs, great and small, of this present-day generation and world of ours: of the many millions who are starving, compared with whom we are getting on well—of the dark threat offered by the atomic bomb to our beautiful earth—of the state of helplessness in which the great statesmen face the task of speaking reasonably to one another—of the pain of the sick and the confusions of the mentally ill— of the widespread failure of our public ordinances and of the folly of most of our habits and customs—of so much pointlessness and useless activity in our intellectual and cultural life—of the uncertainty and weakness too of our church life—of so much grief and confusion in our families, and finally too of all the particular sorrows and burdens which may afflict each one of us today.

Now we pray to you: Lord, let it be day! Lord, shatter, break, destroy all the power of darkness! Heal us, Lord, then we shall be whole!—if this cannot be done entirely yet, then do it in small and passing things as a sign that you are alive and that we, in spite of everything, are your people whom you are leading through everything towards your glory! You alone are good! You alone deserve honour! You alone can and will help! Only we must learn once again to shout with all our souls: You alone! Amen.

CARRY!

---

19 May 1963

Heavenly father, our life is so mixed up: show us the order which you gave it at first, and want to give back to it! Our thoughts are so scattered: collect them round about your truth! Our way seems so dark before us: go in front of us with the light you have promised us! Our consciences accuse us: let us recognize that we may stand up to serve you and our neighbour! Our hearts are restless within us: Lord, give us your peace!

You are the source of everything good, you are yourself goodness, beside which there is no other. To understand that still more thoroughly, to confess it more sincerely, we have come together at this morning hour. You do not wish to have each one of us seeking you for himself and trying to settle his problems for himself. You want us in our misery and in our hope to be a united people of brothers. As such a people, we now give one another our hands to thank you in common and to stretch out to you these hands of ours, which are repeatedly so empty. Do properly the things that we may do wrongly even during this Sunday task of ours. Speak with us in such a way that in our utter weakness we may, can and must hear you.

In the name and at the bidding of our Lord Jesus, your dear son, we pray: Our Father . . .

Carry one another's loads, and in this way you will fulfil the law of Christ.

GALATIANS 6.2

My dear friends! In Germany there used to be—I don't know if it is still the same today—some remarkable fourth class railway carriages in which for instance country people going to market could spread out and stack their baskets, sacks and the like and which therefore carried outside the sign 'For travellers with heavy loads'. It is really the lot of all of us to be such 'Travellers with heavy loads'. Some know this, others don't. Some are like this openly, others in secret. Some do not notice it till later, when they reach the years of which we say: 'I have no pleasure in them', others manage to feel it even in their youth. Some of these travellers have cheerful faces, others ill-tempered and sad faces. But they all have their loads. At a first hearing that does not seem to be very good. And now this fact pursues us in our text even as far as this Sunday morning—though in a very strange form: 'Carry one another's loads'. But notice: this might mean something very fine. The continuation sounds promising enough: 'And in this way you will fulfil the law of Christ'.—Let us think over what all that means for us.

Let us begin, as is quite often advisable in explaining the Bible, at the *end,* so that starting from there we may understand the beginning.

A *'law'* is spoken about in the text. That too does not sound particularly good, because it reminds us unpleasantly of letters of the alphabet, sentences, paragraphs, to which we ought to stick but which we prefer occasionally to ignore or avoid, with which we can easily come into conflict, and by whose immense power we can be crushed. But we are not talking of just any law, but of a very particular one, namely the 'Law of *Christ'*. Let us notice carefully at once that it does not say: you *shall* fulfil it—which leaves it an open question whether we want to do it or are merely able to do it. It says, as if it were the most natural thing in the world, 'You *will* fulfil it'. And let us consider what our Lord Jesus said himself about this law of his: 'Take my yoke upon you ... and you will find rest for your souls ... For my yoke is easy and my load is light'. That changes the picture. Obviously no excessive demand is made on anybody. No grounds for refusing are possible. Nobody is going to be crushed here. It seems a good, joyful thing to be obedient. It smacks of freedom.

The law of Christ is in fact the law of God's *grace* that is *free* and *sets free*. Jesus Christ has established and enforced this law (and so it is called *his* law). But that took place in what he did and still does as God's son and ambassador and in what he did and does in God's name for the world: that is, for its reconciliation with God and for each one of us, for our salvation. He *did* this and still *does* it as the *great*, the incomparable carrier of loads, who is the only one of his kind. It was in this role that John the Baptist saw him: 'Behold, the Lamb of God, who carries away the sin of the world'. What happened was that all the sins, the offences, mistakes, confusions and perversities of the whole world in all generations and in all countries (including our own!) were loaded upon him as if he had made himself responsible for them. What happened was that he did not complain at the sight of this sea of horrors and did not protest at the unheard-of demands made upon him, but instead took all this load willingly upon himself and let our sin be his sin, our grief his grief. What happened was that he carried all this load: 'carried it up to the cross', as we read in another place. What happened was that, by dying on the cross, he carried the load away, removed it and did away with it—and *set free* the world and all of us from it. This really happened.

But something more happened: it was as the great carrier of loads and so as the one who puts into effect the almighty love with which God loved the world and us too, that he rose from the dead and lives, shines and rules for ever, to all eternity. As such he became and is Lord and Ruler, King and Judge: not as a violent conqueror but as the great carrier of loads. As such he has made the world his kingdom and his property, and has called all of us to be members of this kingdom. It is as such that he says what order and disorder are, decides what is just and unjust, good and evil. It is as such that he gives the world, and us too, his law. As our *Liberator,* then, he became, and is, our *Lawgiver.* And what his law requires from us, prescribes for us and commands us, is simple: it is that we may, and ought to live as people set free by him, the great carrier of loads. For this reason he calls his yoke easy and his load light. For this reason the summons to keep his law is followed at once by the promise: 'And you will find rest for your souls'.

But now let's go back to the *beginning* of our text and so to ourselves, the *carriers of small loads.* We can be, and shall always remain, only carriers of *small* loads: not to be compared with him —either in what we are or in what we may and can do. Ours will be no divine work, but never more than very modest and very feeble human work. What we manage to carry will certainly never be the whole world's load of sin: with the merest shadow of some of the tiniest parts of the load which he carried and still carries, we shall have quite enough to carry. It is not granted to us even to remove that much: it is only as people set free by him that we are allowed to go about with this shadow of a load. But this much we *are* allowed to do. And that is what the law of Christ, what he, the great carrier of huge loads, wishes from us humble carriers of small loads, what he prescribes for us and commands us to do.

But what are the *loads* which *we* are allowed to carry? I called them mere shadows just now. Perhaps it is better to say: they are a sort of hangover produced because in a world whose load of sin Jesus Christ has carried away up to the Cross, we, though set free by him, again and again are given to backsliding at all the wrong times: to backsliding into the old, decaying errors and spites, the perverse and mean actions, into the long since superseded works and practices of arrogance, laziness, lying. It is as if somebody whose arm, broken last autumn, has long since been beautifully healed must now and again (let's say every time the weather changes) remember that something has happened to him. There they are again, quite inexplicable and incomprehensible: the big and little sins, although they were long since thrown into the fire by Jesus Christ and done away with, although we might quite simply and naturally be living in the knowledge that we have been forgiven them. There they are again, ghosts senselessly and wantonly conjured up by us, the ghosts of our past, the time *before* the birth of Christ. Their effects are the loads which we have to carry.

But now we come to the most remarkable feature of our text. It is *not* our *own* loads that we are told to carry, but each is to carry the load of the *other* fellow. Certainly our own sins, and so our loads, are included. And certainly much should be said about dealing with them. But according to our text, which we are now trying to follow, our concern for them is not the characteristic and decisive thing in our obedience to the law of Christ. The important thing is rather to be ready and willing to carry *somebody else's* load and then really to carry it.

Yes, this *somebody else*: your fellow man, your neighbour, this man who is only too near you, with whom you have to live now, or continually or perhaps all your days. O this somebody else with his backsliding and the bad habits he holds on to, haunting you like a ghost in everything he does, in his speech, actions and behaviour! O how he springs up before your eyes, how he deafens your ears, how he forces his way even into your dreams and disturbs your thoughts and wastes your time! O how he gets on your nerves! What a useless specimen he is of those folk who have no inclination to use the freedom given to them! How burdensome he is to you: this fellow-traveller with his heavy load, his baskets and sacks! How hard he makes things for you!— What is to be done in such a nasty situation? Will you ignore him, get out of his way, despise him? Well, if you do that you

won't make any difference: not in him and not for you. You
have scarcely ignored him when he is there again in some shape
or form, just as a fly that you chase away comes buzzing back
again and again. Or will you give him a lecture and tell him what
a man he is, or argue with him, or flatten him with your talk?
This way, as we all like to do, you may get things off your chest a
bit—but in doing so you make things worse for the other fellow.
He stays the same. His loads remain too. And the bother which he
is preparing for you remains the same too. Or do you feel like
punishing him, paying him back in his own coin—as the song
says: What you do to me, I'll do back to you? Dear me, what are
we coming to? Without backsliding yourself, without speaking
and acting like one of these ghosts yourself, you will certainly
never see the end of it. And so really nothing can or will be made
different or better like this. In fact, in *all* these ways nothing can
or will come of it except this: it will be clearly seen that you at
least are just as useless a specimen as the other man of those folk
who, though set free, are still such slaves. What good will come
of this? In all these ways the trouble can only become worse.

Our text shows us a *better* way. *Carry*, so it says, *each one* of you
—the *other* fellow's load.

This is the better way because it honestly takes for granted that
each party is in the same boat, that they belong closely together
and are mutually responsible. *Both* are obviously backsliders and
so carriers of loads. *Both*, too, seem burdensome to each other.
And so both can only be helped *together*. But in this way they
can and are to be helped. Together and not each for himself they
are therefore addressed and called to a common effort: *Carry!*

And above all, the way pointed out here is better because with
it both are called to meaningful, *helpful*, promising activity. Not
to some large-scale, not to some radically beneficial activity:
nobody can remove the loads of the other fellow or the annoyance which this fellow is preparing for him. He *must* not even
have the slightest wish to get rid of this annoyance. *Carrying*

means just this: putting up with the mutual annoyance, suffering it, enduring it patiently. *Carrying* means: making use of the permission and opportunity to excuse the annoyance each causes the other. *Carrying* means: treating each other with a little kindness, not as we would treat rough, wicked men, but as we would treat poor, sick ones—rather like the way that seems natural to patients in the same room in a hospital. So *carrying* is really the opposite of blindness and indifference to the backsliding and sin of which both are guilty, and also the opposite of all the irritated accusations and brawls that start up at the sight of them. *Carrying* consists of the help given mutually when people receive and accept each other, together with each other's load, as comrades on a journey that they have begun together and can only continue together and end together. Certainly *carrying* will then quite definitely include discovering the beam in your own eye and finding that it is far more interesting than the mote in your brother's eyes; it will include being ready to look ten times harder for guilt, and so for the need of pardon, in yourself than in the other fellow. In this way we help one another and as a result each one helps himself. In this way we both get things off our chest, while any other way can only lead to new misery. In this way things get changed—not all of them, but at any rate some of them.

It is only a *small* step in the right direction that we carriers of *small* loads can decide to make here and in fact make. But this small step in the right direction brings with it—now we are once again coming to the *end* of our text—the great *promise*, which any other activity, even the most grandiose, does not bring: 'And in this way you will fulfil the law of Christ'.

By carrying one another's loads, you are in fact doing something which, though not the same as his activity as the great carrier of loads, is still similar to it and corresponds to it like a reflection or echo. We can put it another way: by acting like this you do on a small scale and in particular cases what he has done and still does on a large scale and universally—he as the Son of God and perfect Saviour, you as his very imperfect human children. By acting like this, practising this sort of carrying, you may become humble before the law of the free and liberating grace that appeared in him, humble but thoroughly obedient. You live and act then by doing this in his company, together with him, as one of his followers: as ones who in spite of their ghost-like existence and all their backsliding are freed of their loads, liberated, saved and preserved for eternal life. You may then join in the hymn:

> Humbly trusting, never doubting,
> I shall never cease from shouting,
> Though still a pilgrim here on earth:
> 'Let every land his glory sing
> And bow before the Lord our King,
> To honour, love and praise his worth!'

However small it may be, in company with the great carrier of loads and in imitation of him it is the very beginning of our participation in *his* glorious fulfilment of the commandment: '*Love* your neighbour as yourself'. Amen.

Lord, you see and experience all the grief on earth and in the lives of all of us: you see how we torture ourselves and others, how we carry on living without one another and even against one another, how we always claim to know best and for that very reason again and again do wrong and cause distress. We thank you not only for having shown us the better way but for having opened it up for us. Give us courage to start out along it and to walk along it and so to make use of the freedom granted us in the sacrifice of your dear son!

Give this courage also to ever-increasing numbers of people and eventually to all: to those who here and everywhere are imprisoned by their own or somebody else's guilt—to those who are too irreligious and those who are too pious—to rich and poor—to those sick and aged in body and soul and to those who are healthy and young, who so easily forget that it will be their turn one day! Give this courage to the members of our administration, courts, newspaper offices—give it to every individual citizen as he carries out his duties and as he exercises his rights in the state and in society! Give it to the people and most particularly to the ministers of our congregations and religious communities of every kind—not least to the Pope and others who these days have to face such important new responsibilities in the Catholic Church! Let us all, even though we are not yet one, be united in the knowledge that we need to be awakened and to turn again to the Gospel—joyfully bearing for one another whatever still hinders us and disturbs us anywhere—praying for your Holy Spirit without whose work and support none of this can take place! To your most faithful concern we commit our ways and the anxieties of our hearts. Amen.

BUT TAKE HEART

24 December 1963

Great and holy God, in your dear son, our Lord Jesus Christ, you came into our midst as one of us, you have become ours, so that we might be utterly yours! So you have given us the permission, the command and the power to know you, to love and praise you.

To do this in common we have gathered this evening before the festival of your birth. We would like to thank you for the work of your almighty mercy. We must certainly confess at once that we, and our thoughts and our words and our life, again and again fall disgracefully short of what you are and what you do for us. And so we can only ask you not to remove your strong and kind hand from us, and still to be our father and brother, Saviour and Lord.

Grant us too at this time something of the incomprehensible and un-deserved grace of your presence! Let us learn in the light of your word and in the power of your spirit to understand you and one another and ourselves a little better, and so let us gain new comfort, new courage, new patience, new hope! Let this take place today and tomorrow every-where where men—whether they know it or not—wait for the mystery of Christmas to be revealed to them as their salvation and their life! Our Father . . . Amen.

In the world you face anxiety; but take heart, I have conquered the world.

JOHN 16.33

My dear friends, we have all come together on this Christmas Eve to prepare ourselves together to hear the Christmas message tomorrow. You know that this time many other people who cannot be seen are listening on the radio as we pray here and sing and have God's Word spoken to us: outside in the city, in the rest of Switzerland, even in great parts of Germany. That ought to please us rather than disturb us. We have just sung 'Now shall the air with shouts declare: Jesus Christ is born'. That is how we greet those who are listening with us.

I have conquered the world. That is the message of Christmas. *I!* The Child in the manger of Bethlehem says this to us—with the greatest humility, but also with the greatest power and emphasis. I, the Son of God, the almighty father, the creator of heaven and earth! I, whom he has given to you men as a son of man like yourselves, so that he may be your God and you may be his people—so that the salvation, the peace, the joy of this covenant may come upon you! *I* have conquered the world. Not you wicked men, nor you good men either, not you foolish nor you clever men, not you believers nor you unbelievers. No Pope and no Council, no government and no university has done this, no science and no technology—even if you were to succeed the day after tomorrow in sledging along the Milky Way. *I* have done it.

I have conquered the *world*. The world is involved in the Christmas message. The world: our great dwelling-house, built and arranged so well and so splendidly as God's creation—and now for all that so full of darkness, a place of so much wrong and sadness. The world: ourselves, we men, also created well by God and intended from the beginning to be his children—and now for all that, fallen away from him, his enemies, and so enemies of one another, and so each his own enemy. It is this very world that God loved so very much and in such a way that he was

willing to bestow on it, and did bestow on it, me, his son—
that's what the child of Bethlehem says.

I have *conquered* the world, says this child. A great Lord was
needed to do this. Yes, but that is what he is. A strange Lord indeed, quite different from the other great lords who claim to be
able to conquer this or that continent, subdue it and bring it under
control by cunning and violence. A Lord who as the child of
poor people was born abroad in a stable, and was laid in a manger
beside an ox and an ass—and who knows if the wood of this
manger was not taken from the same forest from which wood
was later hewn again to build a cross? For this child has conquered
the world by letting himself be delivered up for its sin and guilt
to the death of shame. This way he snatched it from ruin. This
way he reconciled it with God. This way he won it for God. This
way he restored it. This way he gave us men back to ourselves
more splendid than before.

I *have* conquered the world, we hear. Not: I shall do it some
day! but: it is finished, it has happened. I have done it. All you
need to do now is to notice, and get ready to accept the fact, that
you are living in a world conquered by me—and are already men
conquered by me.

That is the Christmas message. To hear it, to let it take effect,
to digest it, to live by it—this is what we wish to prepare ourselves for together on this Christmas Eve: I have conquered the
world.

But wait. If he, Jesus Christ, did not tell us this, it might seem
too good to be true. But he is the very one who tells us, just as
we heard—first of all, in fact—something else quite different:
In the world you face anxiety.

In German '*Angst*' (anxiety) has a good deal to do with '*Enge*'
(tightness). Anxiety is constriction, oppression, affliction by
some danger that threatens us. And now the Lord does not tell us
that we might face or should or ought to face anxiety. Nor does

he reproach us for being anxious. He simply states it as a plain fact: In the world you face anxiety.

Would we perhaps prefer not to hear anything on this subject? Do we think perhaps: that has nothing to do with Christmas time, or our Christmas carols, Christmas lights and Christmas presents? Let us beware, my friends: our whole Christmas atmospere could be dishonest, a great delusion, if we were unwilling to listen to this as well: In the world you face anxiety. It is the child in the manger at Bethlehem, it is the man who was nailed to the Cross on Golgotha who tells us both things: I have conquered the world—*and:* In the world you face anxiety. If we were to try to shut our ears to the second statement, then we would not hear or understand the first. So let us listen without offence when we are told: We face anxiety—even the strong men among us, even now, even on this Christmas Eve.

There is anxiety that affects many young people: anxiety about themselves, about the life in front of them with its uncanny difficulties, which they are perhaps just beginning to suspect, or which they already know only too well.

There is anxiety that affects old people: anxiety about the increase in their bodily and mental ailments and infirmities—the thought that their whole future might now lie behind them and that they might no longer be of use for anything.

There is at all ages an anxiety called claustrophobia: fear of people, perhaps particularly of those closest to us who always want something, always encroach too much—fear of the crowding in of the many, in whose midst one curiously enough feels utterly lonely and lost.

There is a well justified anxiety about heavy responsibilities which can be placed upon us: I need not hide from you the fact that for as long as I can remember, every time when I am to preach, and so too yesterday and today, I have felt anxious.

There is—this too is a very serious thing—anxiety in the face of the continual passage of time, of the days, weeks and years of this our one and only short life. Does it not seem as if we spent this time just gossiping? Is it not as if we were running away from it?

And then there is anxiety at events threatening us with danger or destruction: such as a fatal illness whose insidious approach we suspect. The unimaginable fear of those eighty people in the air-craft crashing at Dürrenäsch in the minutes and seconds when they could not fail to notice what inevitably faced them—and likewise the fear of the people in Skopje when the earth tremors came, one after the other—and likewise the fear of the people in the Piave valley when the dam burst and the floods broke through to engulf whole villages.

And were we not seized too with great anxiety a month ago when the shattering news of the murder of the American President came through—and the next day the distasteful news of the murder of his murderer: anxiety at what was now to take place, and simply the anxiety at the grim possibilities which obviously may really take place in the life of human society at any moment?

Does it not arouse anxiety in us to see how certain errors and lies which had been thought to be overcome, perhaps overcome for centuries, break out afresh and gather strength in the history of mankind, even among Christians? Does not the thought some-times force itself on us that we might be living in one great mad-house—and is that not a thought that arouses anxiety?

And of course we live in constant anxiety over the atomic bomb, about which so many people nowadays are troubled either openly or in secret and about which one would earnestly wish that many more people might be deeply troubled. It is all very well now that there is an agreement that further experi-ments with this devilish device are to be carried out in future only under the ground. And it is all very well that according to the resolutions of last week even our own dear Switzerland has associated itself with this agreement. But are not too great stocks of this devilish device already available in various places which are sufficient to wipe out all life on our planet many times over?

And does not the whole business painfully remind us of the story we can find in the works of Jeremias Gotthelf about the black spider, bringing death in its wake, which had indeed been carefully kept in a hole in the wall sealed with a plug, until one day a fool came along, tore out the plug and gave free vent to destruction? We have often been very wisely taught that nowadays we must simply 'live with the bomb'. That's all very well, but it still means that nowadays we must live with this particular anxiety.

Another thing: might not one or other of you people even face anxiety about the very festival of Christmas itself: anxiety about the painful memory of previous, better Christmas days—anxiety about the loneliness which you might have to put up with at Christmas—anxiety about the invitation to be cheerful today, when you cannot be cheerful at all—anxiety about God, with whom we get on very familiar and plain-speaking terms at Christmas and yet with whom we are so very far from being in the clear?

In short, it is like this: in the world you face anxiety. Of course we also need the word of the Lord for us to admit this and give it proper consideration. But it is like this and we now can sum up everything that I have merely hinted at under one head: we are anxious to face life, which can just as well be called being anxious to face death, because the great anxiety that threatens us is that we shall find our life surrounded by death, by utter extinction looming up on all sides, and by the nothingness to which life is subjected without hope of being saved. We are afraid of the night when no one can work. Certainly there are all sorts of little, unnecessary, passing anxieties, but strictly speaking they too are signs, as it were, symptoms of the great anxiety to face life and death which affects us all: deeply hidden perhaps, but affecting all of us.

Dear friends, to Christmas Eve, to our preparation for hearing the message of Christmas belongs a duty that we cannot shirk, namely to accept and admit that in the world we face anxiety.

.   .   .

But enough now on this subject! The same person who tells each one of us that we face anxiety in the world, the child in the manger and the man on the Cross, goes on to say, indeed to shout unmistakeably into all the restless sea of our anxiety: *But take heart.*

Here we have it once again: the powerful, glorious *But!*, which we meet in so many other places in the Bible as well. Something undeniably and unshakeably true is given us here to remember at all times, such as: With men this is impossible. Or: The mountains shall depart, and the hills be removed. Or: Heaven and earth shall pass away. Or: The Lord has disciplined me severely. But then a second statement is set against this, which though not denying the first one and so not cancelling and wiping it out, suddenly makes it seem trivial for all that and overshadows it. For instance: But with God all things are possible. Or: But my kindness shall not depart from you. Or: But my words shall not pass away. Or: But he has not given me over unto death. So in this case also: In the world you face anxiety. *But take heart.*

'Take heart' does not mean: Just think of something else. Jump across the thing that is causing you anxiety. Run away from your anxiety—to some amusement or to some feverish activity or to some wild undertaking. You can and will not escape from it any more than you can escape from yourselves. And be careful: this very attempt to run away from anxiety, utterly impossible and useless as it is, for some reason or other is regularly the cause of all evil and all new suffering.

Take heart means: open your eyes and look up: to the hills from whence comes your aid—and look forwards: to the few paces you can take on your way now without hindrance. And then walk on with firm steps: Then take courage. Then even cheer up a bit—right where you are, in the middle of the anxiety, the great anxiety, about facing life and death which no doubt troubles you.

Yes, but can we do this? Is this any more than a word of advice and encouragement given by a well-meaning man which for all that nobody can use in practice, or do anything at all with? The answer is: Certainly *nobody on his own resources*, with his own inventiveness, understanding and powers of decision, can want to take heart, let alone take heart. Everybody without exception can, however, take heart if he listens to the word telling him that he can and must take heart, when it is spoken to him by the one who himself, as true son of God and son of man, came into the world in which we face anxiety. In the midst of it all he himself felt the greatest anxiety—'My God, my God, why have you abandoned me?'—but he has conquered this world, reconciled it with God, and so set a limit to the anxiety which we experience. From this limit set by him there shines forth to us, the people that walk in darkness, a great light. By seeing this light, following this light—by looking towards him who makes it shine upon us, by holding fast to him, by believing in him as we say—we have his word that we shall be free to take heart: free to be set at rest, not before the storm, nor after the storm, but right in the middle of the storm of our anxiety, 'when we are in direst distress and do *not* know where to turn'.

So the question whether we can take heart as the Lord orders us really needs a second answer. Just as no one can take heart by himself, so too he can't take heart *for himself alone*. But each one without exception can certainly take heart, if he lets himself be included among the race of people to which it is said, not privately to this or that one, but in the belonging together of all its members, that it may and must take heart: to the race of people on which, in the darkness of its anxiety to face life and death, the great light shines. But can you really hear in the middle of anxiety the angels singing and saying: Glory to God in the highest? Try it out this way: you can, if you listen also to the rest of what they sang and said: Peace on earth! Peace even in this building! Peace between you and the person who sits next to you or behind you on the bench! Peace between the man in this cell and the one in that cell! Peace between the prisoners and the warders! And peace between each one here and his relatives at home! Can you really manage to look up and to look forward? You can, by not failing to look to left and right at your neighbours who would also like to look up and look forward and who perhaps only need your assistance to do so. Could you really hold fast to Jesus Christ as your Saviour and believe in him? You will do it by finding in those around you, whether you like or dislike them, not a mass of miscellaneous 'people' but the community loved and called by Jesus Christ who is the Saviour of them all.

Is it quite certain that even you may call yourself a child of God and in fact be one in the midst of the world and so in the midst of anxiety? You may and must most certainly call yourself one and be one by treating others as your brothers, because they are also brothers of Jesus Christ and so children of God. This is at all times and for all of us the test of our faith. But why should we fail this test?

So let us on this Christmas Eve prepare ourselves to hear that, in the midst of the anxiety which afflicts us, we may, must and also can take heart. And to listen when we are told that we are allowed to hear this in company with all those to whom the same Lord and Saviour has also said it, and will say it again.

Every year we celebrate Christmas Eve afresh. We are celebrating it today just as we celebrated it last year and as we shall celebrate it next year as well, if we are still alive; and each time on the following day we celebrate Christmas. Let me add just one last thing. You know that our whole life in time may and must really be one long Christmas Eve preparing us for the one, great and final, eternal Christmas, which is the goal of all God's ways with mankind and of all his ways too with each single one of us. So I shall now read a few more verses from the end of the last book of the Bible which deal with this eternal Christmas: 'Then I saw a new heaven and a new earth, for the first heaven and the first earth had vanished, and there was no longer any sea. And I John, saw the holy city, new Jerusalem, coming down out of heaven from God, made ready like a bride adorned for her husband. I heard a loud voice proclaiming from the throne: 'Now at last God has his dwelling among men! He will dwell among them and they shall be his people, and God himself will be with them. He will wipe every tear from their eyes; there shall be an end to death, and to mourning and crying and pain; for the old order has passed away!" Then he who sat on the throne said, "Behold! I am making all things new!"' Amen.

O Lord Jesus Christ, if everything is not to be worthless, then you yourself must come to us and speak to us of the glory of what you were for us and did for us, and still are and still do and will again be and again do—and of the sober truth that in the world we face anxiety—above all, however, of the joyful hope by which we may now and for ever hold fast to you. We are such poor, deaf and dumb people. Open our ears so that we can hear you—and our mouths so that we can bear witness to you for one another!

Speak your word to all of us so that, called together by you, we may become utterly your people, utterly your community! Tell it to each one so that he is not only called a Christian but may again and again become one afresh. Tell it too to all our relatives at home! Tell it to all the prisoners in all the prisons in every corner of the earth! Tell it to the sick, the suffering, the dying across there in the hospitals! Tell it to all the crowd of people who are excited, worried and weary! Tell it to the sad and the spiteful, those who are too superficial and too thoughtful, too religious and too irreligious! Tell it to parents and children, teachers, writers and newspaper correspondents, the members of our administrative authorities and courts, the ministers and their congregations, the great and strong and the humble and weak of all races! We all need to hear you telling us this as only you can tell us. And so grant us all a

*good Christmas: tomorrow and at the goal and end of our days and the
days of all men!*

*Christ, you Lamb of God, who carry away the sins of the world, have
mercy upon us, grant us your peace! Amen.*

WHEN THEY SAW THE LORD

Easter 29 March 1964

Dear Lord, almighty God and father! If only we would properly acknowledge what you did for your people, for the whole world and so too for us by raising Jesus Christ, your son, our brother from among the dead whom even he had joined, and by clothing him with everlasting life for your glory and our salvation! If only we were properly grateful for the promise, the comfort and the guidance which you have given once and for all in this way to us, the rest of mankind! If only we would accept it and in all that we are and think and say and do show that Easter day is the true birthday of all of us, a day alongside which all our other days may be set as days of freedom, peace and joy!

Let us remember something of this when at this hour we come together to try to declare your word and to hear it! You know that even our deepest sincerity and enthusiasm, even our greatest attention, cannot ensure that we become a proper Easter congregation. The light that is needed for this here, as in all the churches in this town and anywhere else, can only come from you yourself. We ask you without any pretension but in childlike trust not to let this light be hidden anywhere, and not among us either. Our Father . . . Amen.

On the evening of that day, the first day of the week, the doors being shut where the disciples were, for fear of the Jews, Jesus came and stood in the midst, and said to them, 'Peace be with you'. And when he had said this, he showed them his hands and his side. Then the disciples became glad when they saw the Lord.
JOHN 20.19–20

My dear friends,

We have come here to celebrate the memory of 'that day', that first day of the week. Instead of the Jewish Sabbath as the seventh day, this first day became the true Sabbath in the Christian community almost by itself, and so was its weekly festival. Its explanation and origin thus lies in that first day. In the Germanic languages it has a rather pagan name: 'Sunday'. Now as on that day the sun of righteousness rose amid the dark world of unrighteousness, it may certainly be called a sun-day even now. But it is better named in the Romance languages as the 'Day of the Lord': because he, the Lord, is the sun of righteousness that rose on that day.

That day was a day like any other in our reckoning of time. What made it 'that day'—that special day—was what happened on it: the resurrection of Jesus Christ from the dead, the raising of this one man who had died, his abduction from the grave into which two days before he had been laid after being crucified and having died.

My dear friends, why could this happen and why did it happen: this conquest and elimination, this death of his death, when he was clothed and invested—not of course with his former mortal life, but with a new immortal one? The reason for this I know no better than you do. Nothing is simpler than to say that you cannot believe it. Even at the time, it could not be told about, let alone described and explained. So there is no place in the New Testament in which such a thing is even attempted. The raising of Jesus was utterly and completely the work of God; as such it was indeed well done but also quite incomprehensible. Even at the time, it could only be recognized, acknowledged, attested and declared that such a thing had taken place. 'Jesus Christ is risen' is how one Christian greets another today in Russia, to which then the other answers: 'He is risen indeed!' But this is the point: that is not describing, it is witnessing and declaring.

The only thing which happened on that day that they managed to describe was what followed the resurrection of Jesus: namely that he appeared to his disciples, that he met them (of course not only in thought, or in a dream or in some mental way, but visible in body, and able to be heard and even touched). This man who earlier had died was now alive in the way that God is alive and was alive in God's power, living directly by him and with him and therefore undying, immortal and incorruptible. It was in this way that Jesus came to his disciples on that day. That much could be clearly told, however stammeringly. And in this narrative there was and is attested and declared, at that time and right to this day, something that could not and cannot be described in words: the resurrection of Jesus.

Well then—as the narrative and the testimony says: 'On the evening of that day Jesus came'. As had been foreseen and expected? No—it was certainly as he had promised earlier on, but how could anybody have taken it in then, let alone have understood it? What a coming! Out from the domain ruled over by the death that controls all men—out from the grave, which has never again given back anybody else who had really died! So it was a coming from a place whence nobody else had come: a coming utterly unforeseen, utterly unexpected. But he, Jesus, came from there. Was he really the same Jesus of Nazareth whom they had known before? Yes, known and yet not at all known as he really was. The same then, but the same now in his glory, that is to say revealing himself as the true son of God and son of man, whom they had not seen before with eyes that saw, or heard with ears that heard. The same then, but now it was that their eyes and ears were opened when he opened them.

This Jesus risen from the dead came and 'stood in the midst'. Let us linger a little over this remarkable statement.

It says of course above all: He came into the midst of his disciples. He came, then, to the very spot which in the long hours since the evening of Good Friday they could only see as empty, where they could only see nothingness: only the memory of his blood-drenched body taken down from the Cross, only his grave and with it only their own past errors and illusions, only the end of all things.

Let us not have any false notions about these disciples of Jesus! They were no more than we a group of pious believers or even of good, brave, worthy people: on that day less than ever. Like a flock of hens on the perch after a thunderstorm they were sitting there—or in more elegant terms: like a little group of children who have just lost their father and mother—or like a troop of soldiers in flight after a defeat. The most terrible thing possible had taken place: the other side had won. Jesus was definitely no longer there. And they themselves? How often had they misunderstood him, and thought, spoken and lived quite differently from the way he had told them. And then when the great test followed, one of their number had betrayed him for thirty pieces of silver. Then they had all left him and had fled. Then their strongest man, the man of rock, Peter, on whom Jesus intended to build his church, had denied him three times. What was to become of them? There they sat behind closed doors: bolted for fear of the Jews, who had condemned Jesus and delivered him up to the heathen so that they might kill him—from fear that the same might happen to them. Repentance, mourning, fear was all that was left to them: a heap of broken fragments. No, these were not saints, not heroes.

To them came the risen Jesus and stepped into their midst.

Why? To make himself, in the might of God's great mercy, the head of this forlorn group, of these miserable and burdened, gloomy and frightened and cowardly men—the head of this thoroughly sick body. He did that in the simplest way imaginable: 'Peace be with you', he said to them and that meant in the language of those days no less, though no more, than when nowadays a person goes up to some others and says: 'Good evening (or good morning), everybody'. In such a human way, so much just one of themselves, he stepped into their midst. But when two people do the same thing it is not the same. Jesus did not just wish peace for his disciples: he brought, indeed created for his disciples what that simple word said: Peace, a good evening, a good day.

He did that by showing them his pierced hands, his wounded side, that is, the marks of his death on the Cross. In so doing he revealed himself not only as the one whose lot it was to be beaten, wounded and killed, but also as the one who had taken all this upon himself in the freedom of his obedience to God his father, and whose very shame God had now made the mark of his glory. It was as the Lamb of God slaughtered on the Cross that he now showed himself to be living, the victorious Lion of Judah: the Saviour of all the world that God loved, and so their Saviour too. In this way the risen Jesus appeared and met his followers: as a prophet of the one unchangeable and infallible truth of God, who now took into his own hands, effectively and once and for all, the instruction, regulation, equipment, leadership of that forlorn group, his people. In this way he made this little people in all its powerlessness mightier than all the nations of the world. In this way he wished, no, brought and created for it peace, a good evening, a good day, by coming into their midst.

But we may and must add something: When he came into their midst he came into the midst of the life of each single one of them, whether he was called Peter or John, Andrew or James. Peace be with you! Good evening, everybody. That meant right away: Peace be with you, my friend. A good new day especially to you! If he died and rose again as the head of his whole body, then he did so also as the head of each of its limbs, he did so also for your justification before God and for the sanctification of your life. If his people, by his coming into their midst, no longer stood in front of his corpse, in front of his grave, no longer in front of a pile of broken fragments then neither do you, but rather you too have been born again by his resurrection to a living hope. If his church as such receives his permission and his command to pray: 'Our Father in Heaven!' then you, my friend, may and shall know that *you* are his dear child. Whatever concerns all men in the meeting of the risen Christ with his disciples most certainly concerns *you*. 'My Lord and my God!' cried Thomas when he recognized him after all the others and with all the others.

But here something more may and must be added: the man who came that day into the midst of his disciples came by that very act into the midst, mounted by that very act the throne that was his by right in the midst of all the world's history. Jesus Christ on that occasion wished, brought and created peace, a good day for all men of all people and times in the whole world, visible and invisible. Into the midst of all humanity now cheering to high Heaven, now grieved to death, right in among all the far too stupid and far too clever people, the far too confident and far too despairing people, in among all the religious and irreligious people, there came in might as the Lord of all of them this Jesus who had been crucified and had risen again. Right into all the illnesses and natural catastrophes, all the wars and revolutions, the making and breaking of peace, all the progress, stagnation and recessions, all the human misery, whether somebody could be blamed for it or not, it came about at the proper time that he showed himself and revealed himself as the one that he was and is and will be: Peace be with you! and he showed them his hands and his side. Among whatever plants and weeds this seed was sown on that day, it is ripening ready for harvesting. Let us depend on this: Whatever happened on that day became, was and remained the centre round which everything else revolves, the point from which everything else comes at first and to which it is hurrying in the end. There are many real and many apparent, many bright and many dim lights: but this one will burn longest, even when all the rest have had their day and are once more put out. For any thing lasts its time, but the love of God which was at work and found expression in the raising of Jesus Christ from the dead, lasts for ever. Because this once happened, there is therefore no reason for despair, there is every reason for hope—even as we read the newspaper with all its confusing and frightening news, even for the story uncannily reflecting so many colours, that we call world history.

So then Jesus, the one great mediator between God and us men, risen from the dead, came into the midst of his people and into the life of every single person and of all the history of the world. So he spoke and so he speaks from there the first and last word. But let us return once more to the disciples on that day, the good day of the Lord, the first Sunday. From them we hear at the end of our text: 'They became glad when they saw the Lord'. That does not mean that now all at once they had nothing more to ask or to complain about, or that at last they had really become great saints and heroes. But it means that they found themselves comforted, encouraged, set on their feet, that they might in all humility lift their heads a little and hold them up. What they heard when they saw the Lord was an irresistible, quite practical appeal, the call to service as his witnesses in the world, among the rest of humanity. What they had there, for all their limitations, was the vision of a clear and crowded future for their existence in time. And what they heard over and above that, when they saw the Lord, was the thin but utterly strong note of eternal hope for themselves and all creation. 'Death, where is your sting? Where, grave, your victory? Thanks be to God who gives us the victory through our Lord Jesus Christ.' They gained a vision of a final breaking of all bonds, of a last and final solution of all riddles, of being recognized and existing in the kingdom of eternal light, whose first ray had touched them and lit their path at that very moment, on that day. For that very reason they became glad when they saw the Lord. That they became glad certainly already meant for them that they might even laugh a little—not at once right over their faces, but continually from then on deep down inside.

Dear friends, we were not there when the risen Jesus, in spite of all the folly and mourning of his disciples, in spite of these doors shut from sheer terror, came into their midst. We cannot see him now as directly as they could, nor shall we be able to see him like that until he comes to judge the living and the dead at the end of all time. But in our way, indirectly, that is in the mirror of the narrative and so of the witness, the confession, the proclamation of the first community, we too can and may see him here and now. Many before us, a whole race of men, have seen him in this and have become glad. For this very reason we celebrate Easter, the festival in memory of that day, to join those people, to see the Lord in that mirror, and so too to become glad. Without seeing the Lord nobody can be glad. Whoever sees him will become glad. Why should this not happen here to us as well, to the little Easter congregation of prisoners in Basel's Spitalstrasse with their chaplain and their organist, with all the inmates and warders of this institution and (after all, I suppose I belong here too) with the old professor who occasionally pays a visit here? All of us can see the Lord too. So all of us may become glad too. God grant that this may happen to us. Amen.

Lord Jesus Christ, you know what it means to be a man and to be in misery. For you have been thrust down, or rather have freely come down, to the lowest depths, and have been abandoned, betrayed, denied, condemned and killed as the greatest of sinners; you have completely become one of the dead in order to become completely our brother. But you know too what it means to be a man with God. As such you have been raised in the power of your father and his holy spirit, and have risen from the dead and have become the light of your people, of each human being and Christian, throughout the world. So you are at work, snatching us from the depths and taking us up to the heights. We thank you for all this. We ask you that all this may not have happened and will not in the future happen in vain.

Together with all those other people who have seen and recognized you as the Lord, we ask you this above all, however, for the sake of the many who have not yet known you or no longer know you as the Lord. Keep our eyes open, and open the eyes of the indifferent, the despairing, the rough and ready and the refined atheists, sceptics or whatever else they care to call themselves, so that they—for basically they are all so sad—may become glad!

Let the light of your resurrection shine in the churches of every kind and denomination, in all the other prisons, in the hospitals and mental hospitals, in the council chambers and council rooms of our administrative authorities, in the editorial offices of our newspapers, in our schools, in all the private houses and families in which there is so much open and hidden need, confusion and worry! In this we think not least of our relatives near and far: be their friend and comforter, their adviser and helper.

And when one day the shadows of death come nearer to all of us, then be and remain the one nearest us, then tell us the one thing which we must hear: that you are alive and that we too shall live! Amen.